EDITOR: LEE JOHNS

CW00665803

OSPREY
MILITARY

MEN-AT-ARMS

THE AUSTRIAN ARMY
1740-80: 1 CAVALRY

Text by
PHILIP HAYTHORNTHWAITE
Colour plates by
BILL YOUNGHUSBAND

First published in Great Britain in 1994
by Osprey, an imprint of Reed Consumer Books Limited
Michelin House, 81 Fulham Road,
London SW3 6RB
and Auckland, Melbourne, Singapore and Toronto

ISBN 1 85532 415 6

Filmset in Great Britain by Keyspools Ltd, Golborne,
Lancashire
Printed through Bookbuilders Ltd, Hong Kong

Artist's note

Readers may care to note that the original paintings
from which the colour plates in this book were
prepared are available for private sale. All
reproduction copyright whatsoever is retained by the
publisher. Enquiries should be addressed to:
    William Younghusband
    12 St Matthew's Walk
    Chapel Allerton
    Leeds LS7 3PS
The publishers regret that they can enter into no
correspondence upon this matter.

Publisher's note

Readers may wish to study this title in conjunction
with the following Osprey publications:
    MAA 236 *Frederick the Great's Army (1) Cavalry*
    MAA 240 *Frederick the Great's Army (2) Infantry*
    MAA 248 *Frederick the Great's Army (3) Specialist
        Troops*

For a catalogue of all books published by Osprey Military
please write to:

**The Marketing Manager,
Consumer Catalogue Department,
Osprey Publishing Ltd,
Michelin House, 81 Fulham Road,
London SW3 6RB**

THE EMPIRE AND ARMY

Austria was both a major participant and one of the causes of hostilities in the wars of the mid-18th century. In one sense, however, 'Austria' is a misnomer, the country representing only a small part of the territories later known as the Austrian Empire. Nor is it correct to use the term 'Holy Roman Empire', for that included a number of autonomous states owing nominal allegiance to the Emperor; and for a short time during the period under review, the Emperor was not the ruling monarch of Austria. It is perhaps more accurate to refer to the Austrian Empire as 'the Habsburg Empire', from the name of the ruling family established in Austria from the 13th century. The death of the Habsburg Emperor Charles VI in October 1740 set in motion the first of the major wars of the mid-18th century: the War of the Austrian Succession. Charles's heir was a daughter, Maria Theresa, whose accession to the Habsburg lands was disputed. She was to become one of the

greatest figures in the history of the 18th century and it is her reign which determines the parameters of the present study.

Kept intact by the Pragmatic Sanction of 1713, despite the lack of a male heir, the Habsburg territories were immense. They were often reckoned to consist of 'German' and 'Hungarian' parts, although such a division is misleading and probably arose from the fact that Hungary was a separate kingdom, thus consigning all other territories to the 'German' part. The true 'German' lands consisted of Austria itself (with the capital at Vienna), and the provinces to the south and west of the Tyrol: Carinthia, Styria and Carniola, extending to the Adriatic at Trieste; there were also small, isolated German enclaves in the west, *Vorder-Osterreich* (literally 'frontal Austria'), of which the most significant was the Breisgau, an area on the right bank of the Rhine in which the Habsburgs first acquired territory in the late 13th century, and then from 1368 the town and countship of Freiburg. To the north of Austria was Bohemia, the kingship to which the Habsburg dynasty had been elected in October 1526, together with its dependent territories of Moravia and Silesia.

At Pressburg the magnates of Hungary swear allegiance to Maria Theresa upon the commencement of her reign, impressed by the bearing of the beautiful young queen, wearing the robes and crown of Hungary, and holding her infant son. (Print after Adolph Menzel)

Maria Theresa: a contemporary print depicting the matronly figure as she appeared in later life.

burgs as kings of Hungary. The country maintained an entirely independent administration and system of government. The latest acquisition was the Bánát, a territory of south-east Hungary north of the Danube, which was captured from the Turks by Eugene of Savoy in 1716, remained under military administration until 1751, and was officially independent of Hungary until 1779. Its name can cause confusion as a *banat* was originally a territory governed by a *ban*, a term for a military governor similar to the original usage of the German *margrave*. It was usual to describe such a territory as 'the banat of . . .'; but when used alone and from the early 18th century, *the* Bánát (Hungarian *Bánság*) described the territory in question, which was governed from Temesvár.

The administration of the Habsburg territories was varied, the Netherlands and Italian provinces governed largely by viceroys of their own nationality, while Hungary remained a sovereign kingdom whose nobility perpetuated a state of feudalism which only grudgingly succumbed to the reforms that Maria Theresa instituted in the rest of the empire. Difficulties arose from the diversity of nationalities within so vast a territory, some mutually distrustful and others inclined to rate their own interests before their allegiance to the ruler.

A number of unifying factors prevented the Habsburg territories from fracturing. Most of the inhabitants were Roman Catholic, a useful factor in maintaining unity as for most of the period the enemy was largely Protestant; indeed, writing of Bohemia and Moravia, Frederick the Great noted that 'the people there are not to be trusted any farther than you can see them . . . The Hussites in the circle [area] of Konigingraetz [Königgrätz] are the only people that can be induced to render us any sort of service'; the remaining Roman Catholic inhabitants he dismissed as 'arrant traitors' whose 'interest is attached to that of the house of Austria'.

Secondly, there was the character of Maria Theresa herself, a quite remarkable woman who, though only 23 at the time of her accession, progressed to become the empire's matriarch, regal yet not demonstrably autocratic like many of her contemporaries. Supported by a happy marriage which produced sixteen children, she exhibited a rare integrity, showing genuine concern for her subjects and a degree of 'enlightenment' which resulted in

Maria Theresa found it impossible to hold the latter against the claims of Frederick the Great of Prussia, and Silesia was lost in 1742.

Also included in the 'German' part of the Habsburg lands were the holdings in Lombardy of the archduchy of Milan, and the duchies of Mantua, Parma and Piacenza. The most recent acquisition was Tuscany, given by treaty to Francis Stephen of Lorraine, in exchange for the ceding of Lorraine to France in 1736, some three months after his marriage to Maria Theresa. Most distant of the 'German' territories were the Austrian Netherlands, approximately the area of modern Belgium and Luxembourg.

The largest of the Habsburg possessions was Hungary, a vast territory which included the Transylvanian border with the Ottoman Empire. Hungary had been acquired progressively from the 16th century onwards, and was held by the Habs-

social reform and strengthened the bonds which held the empire together.

A third unifying force on the Habsburg territories was the army. The 'Austrian' army of the period embraced all nationalities and drew its personnel from the Habsburg lands and beyond. While none of the component provinces maintained an independent military establishment, many units had a distinct national identity, yet one subservient to the wider identity of the Habsburg army, which but for a short period was also that of the Empire.

The provinces did not all contribute to the army in proportion to their wealth or population. The 'Austrian' units relied heavily upon recruits from outside the Habsburg lands, largely from the many independent German states; Bohemia and Moravia were a fruitful source of recruits, the Netherlands provided excellent material, and Lombardy also contributed. Conversely, the independently minded Hungarian magnates provided a disproportionately small amount of resources compared to the size of their territory, although their hussars were originally the army's only light cavalry. The eastern border of Hungary was occupied by Transylvania (*Siebenbürgen*); administered from Vienna it provided only a limited number of recruits. The southern edge of Hungary, known as the 'military borders', drew from Croatia and Slavonia the valuable frontier (*Grenz*) units of 'Croats' and 'Pandours'. Added to these were considerable numbers of foreigners, from whom a number rose to high command, chief among them being the Irish, a nation which provided literally hundreds of officers. Not all these were new immigrants: for example, those who rose to the highest distinction included the Field-Marshals Maximilian Ulysses Browne, mortally wounded at Prague in 1757, who was the son and nephew of distinguished officers in Austrian service; Franz Moritz Lacy, one of the most influential figures in the later Theresian army, who though a member of a Limerick family,

was born in St. Petersburg, the son of the Russian marshal Peter Lacy; and Gideon Ernst Loudon, another major personality, descended from a Scottish family resident in Livonia.

The diverse origins of the members of the army caused problems, including dislikes and jealousies (most evident between Hungarians and 'Germans'). The difficulties inherent in a force whose native tongues included German, French, Flemish, Italian, Czech, Hungarian, Serbo-Croat, and Latin – used for Hungarian government business – are obvious. Some foreign officers never became fully conversant in German, the most essential language, but as French was familiar to most educated Europeans, commanders usually made themselves understood no matter which troops were under their command. The Prince de Ligne identified various qualities required of a general leading different nations: when commanding an army 'composed of lively materials, such as are to be found among the English, the Italians, the French, and the Hungarians, it must be his study to repress his own ardour, in order to keep under the natural effervescence of his followers. When a man is put at the head of an army made up of colder elements, such as Germans, Bohemians, Russians, or Dutchmen, he

Trooper, Cuirassier Regt. Hohenzollern-Hechingen (no. 3), painted by David Morier, c. 1748. Note the carbine and picket-stake carried at the right of the saddle, the brass fittings of the carbine-belt, and the drum-shaped canteen. Facings and breeches are red, belts buff, the horse-furniture red with white lace with black and red design, and black and white quartered shield; the holster-caps have brown bearskin covers. (The Royal Collection © 1993 Her Majesty the Queen)

must, like Prometheus, endeavour to steal a spark of celestial animation, to give them motion and activity'.

The army's sense of unity was probably considerably reinforced at the beginning of Maria Theresa's reign, when the Habsburgs briefly lost the imperial mantle. In 1742 Elector Charles Albert of Bavaria secured his election as Emperor Charles VII, which reduced Maria Theresa to the status of Archduchess of Austria and Queen of Hungary, and in a state of war with the imperial authority which had been wielded by her father. Under these circumstances the Habsburg army assumed a more national than imperial identity, which can only have been beneficial to morale and the army's sense of unity. Upon Charles Albert's death in 1745, Maria Theresa's husband was elected emperor, restoring the title *kaiserlich und königliche* ('imperial and royal') to the army, and the imperial authority remained in Habsburg hands thereafter. Francis Stephen died in 1765, and from that date Maria Theresa's eldest son, Joseph II, became joint ruler until her death in 1780.

The performance of the Austrian army during Maria Theresa's reign was mixed; considerable victories were counterbalanced by notable defeats, and while a degree of mutual exhaustion hastened the end of the Seven Years' War, Austrian prestige was greater at the conclusion of it than at the beginning of Maria Theresa's reign. Although Austria was not able to recover Silesia, the army had withstood and not infrequently beaten an army that was reckoned to be the best in Europe, a force commanded by one of the 'great captains': Frederick the Great. Perhaps more important was that under Maria Theresa's leadership, the Habsburg empire emerged from the war in a more cohesive state than when she had ascended the throne, with a popular monarchy whose succession was assured. In the brief War of the Bavarian Succession (1778–9), waged by a new generation of Austrian commanders and somewhat against Maria Theresa's more liberal ideas, the army more than held its own and compelled the Prussians to withdraw.

ARMY ORGANISATION

The army was recruited through a combination of voluntary enlistment and conscription. Despite a sophisticated higher administration, the primary responsibility for recruiting lay with the individual regiment. Although fixed recruiting districts were not allocated to individual regiments until 1766, the national identity of the various corps led to the recruiting of men from their own area. However, except for the regiments recruited from Hungarians, men from virtually any part of Europe might be enrolled, as there were few restrictions on the nature of foreigners recruited (although the French and Turks were widely regarded as the least acceptable). Although the 'foreign' element was considerable, the term can be deceptive, as a German from outside the Habsburg territories, though officially 'foreign', might be much less foreign in behaviour and outlook than a Transylvanian or Milanese from within the empire. During the period of hostility with Bavaria and Saxony the number of foreign recruits fell, as these areas were no longer available as a plentiful source of men.

Regimental recruiting-parties offered a cash bounty for those who chose to enlist; cavalry recruits often receiving double that offered to infantrymen. As the cavalry was regarded as especially favoured, recruiters were able to select men who already possessed some knowledge of horses; those eligible were aged between 18 and 40, with a minimum height of 5 feet 4 inches. Although the traditional method of assembling troops in Hungary was by a feudal levy or 'Insurrection', the regiments organised for the army

Cuirassier equipment c. 1760, including a shabraque and holster-caps with double-eagle device, and a pre-1769 sabre with shell-guard. (Print after R. von Ottenfeld)

were formed on regular lines, like those from the 'German' part of the empire.

Voluntary enlistment was supplemented by a limited conscription which applied to the Austrian and Bohemian lands. Initially the term of enlistment was for life (or until the soldier was too infirm to be of use), but in an attempt to encourage the enlistment of a superior calibre of recruit, 'limited service' was introduced from May 1757, by which men could choose to enrol for six years or the duration of hostilities. Eventually up to one-third of the army was composed of 'limited service' men, among whom, it was found, a higher proportion were suited to be NCOs. Only at the very end of Maria Theresa's reign was more widespread conscription instituted. Men selected were trained for two years and then released to pursue their civilian vocations, reporting for only six weeks' training per year. This system never extended to Italy or the Netherlands, and was only later applied to Hungary and the Tyrol, and existed alongside the previous methods of recruiting; it only came into effect in 1781, the year after Maria Theresa's death.

Two other types of 'foreign' soldier fought under Imperial colours. States owing allegiance to the emperor contributed units to the *Reichsarmee* in time of war (such units formed the imperial contribution to the Franco-Allied army at Rossbach, for example); and to remedy shortages of manpower during the Seven Years' War, Austria hired a number of foreign regiments, including Italians (one cavalry and three infantry regiments from Modena in 1757, and the Tuscan regiment taken over in the same year) and Germans such as the two Würzburg regiments taken into Austrian pay in late 1757.

Discipline in the Austrian army was necessarily strict, but nothing like as brutal as that which turned Prussian soldiers into virtual automata (from 1757, for example, it was no longer permitted for Austrian officers or NCOs to kick a man or to batter his head with a stick!). If the conditions of service were less forbidding than those of the Prussian army, the results were mixed; if the Austrians generally lacked the almost unnatural Prussian steadiness under fire, they probably maintained a higher sense of loyalty and were certainly less prone to desertion.

Officers

The origins of the officer corps were as diverse as those of the other ranks. As a rudimentary example, it is interesting to consider the names of those who held the colonelcies of regular regiments during Maria Theresa's reign. It is difficult in some cases to identify the exact origin of a name, and some of those with foreign names came from families resident for many generations in their adopted country; nevertheless, it is interesting to observe that, excluding members of the imperial family and those of the ruling houses of other states, less than 43 per cent of regimental colonels (*Inhabers*) had German names. Other names included 35 Hungarian, 17 French, 17 Italian, 14 Netherlandish, eight Irish, eight Spanish, three Scottish and three Polish; and this does not take into account the several cases of one family name being shared by several *Inhabers*. (Obviously many of the 'French' names originated in the Habsburg possessions in the Netherlands.)

The officer corps was not the socially exclusive élite as in some armies, for although the nobility and the wealthy generally had an easier path to promotion, an officer of lowly birth could rise from the lowest ranks to the highest on merit alone. Initially

Cuirassier officer (left) and trooper, evidently of Regt. Stampa (no. 23) from the green facings and yellow buttons, as decreed in 1765; the uniform is that replaced by the pattern of 1769. (Print after R. von Ottenfeld)

Carabinier in full field equipment, c. 1770, the uniform resembling that of cuirassiers. An iron-shod picket-stake is carried at the right of the saddle. (Print after R. von Ottenfeld)

most officers joined their regiments at an early age as a cadet (of which various grades existed), and were trained by the regiment before receiving the rank of ensign (*Fähnrich*, or *Cornet* for cavalry). Training began to be regularised in 1752 when the Military Academy at Wiener Neustadt was opened, graduates of which were to fill one-third of a regiment's new commissions. Half the Academy students were the offspring of the nobility, and half the sons of distinguished officers or civilian officials, thus enjoying not only superior training but also social advantages over the ordinary regimental cadets, and an easier route to promotion. Company officers were promoted by their regimental colonel, and senior ranks by the empire's Council of War (*Hofkriegsrath*), the latter demanding a payment from the officer for each promotion. Although wealth was not a necessity for promotion, and the officer had to be deemed worthy of advancement, an element of purchase had begun to intrude. The Prince de Ligne remarked that the system of purchase, though not official, had gained ground and in some ways had

been found 'beneficial to the interior economy of corps' and supported the practice against those who regarded it as unfair on the long-serving or wounded officer who could be overtaken by the rich and young.

Although potentially unfair upon the less-favoured, accelerated promotion (by whatever means) did enable officers of talent to attain high rank at a relatively early age; Franz Moritz Lacy, for example, was a full colonel at age 25 and a lieutenant-general (*Feldmarschall-Lieutenant*) at 32. Advancement by seniority alone could be more damaging to the service; a story told to illustrate the point concerned a newly promoted colonel who announced to Count Guido Stahremberg that the emperor had made him a general. The Count corrected him: 'He has *nominated* you a General; but I defy him to make you one!'

Conversely, nobility itself was no guarantee of wealth or influence, for deserving officers, irrespective of social origin, could be given a grant of nobility for distinguished service and, from 1757, for thirty years' good conduct. As this grant brought with it no land, the resulting class of nobility owed their entire existence to their monarch, which solidified the loyalty which was already present among the officer class. Consequently, the army's officers were drawn from origins as diverse as ex-NCOs, the sons of the middle class or minor officials, small landowners and soldiers-of-fortune, as well as from the more 'natural' leaders of society, the sons of officers and the landed nobility, dynasties which ruled their vassals with almost regal authority, and who formed one of the great supports of the monarchy. Nor was there discrimination against foreign officers, for although Hungarian regiments were officered largely by Hungarians, they were in no sense inferior to their 'German' comrades.

The *Inhaber*

At the head of every regiment was the *Inhaber*, a 'colonel-proprietor' who initially enjoyed almost complete control over regimental affairs, including finances, discipline, training, uniform and the right to select and promote officers. The latter was often delegated to the colonel in actual command of the regiment, for the *Inhaber* rarely led his regiment in person, and then generally only by coincidence, if as a general he happened to find his regiment under his immediate command. As the virtual 'owner' of the regiment, the *Inhaber* could use it as a source of revenue in various ways, although a conscientious *Inhaber* might actually lose money by the proper maintenance of his regiment. His powers declined during the period, as various functions were regulated by central authority; from 1765, for example, the *Hofkriegsrath* assumed the right to appoint field officers, and more standard methods of training were introduced, so that by about 1770 the role of the *Inhaber* had become more that of a colonel-in-chief.

The *Inhaber* gave his regiment his name, so regimental designations altered with every change of *Inhaber*. Some regiments kept the same *Inhaber* throughout the period under review, and thus the same name; others might be known by up to five names during the forty years. Even more confusing were those cases in which more than one *Inhaber* bore the same surname (Emerich, Joseph, Nikolaus and Paul Anton Esterházy, for example), and where an *Inhaber* moved from one regiment to another. For example (using the numbering of 1769), 'Cuirassier Regiment Jacquemin' was the title of Regt. No. 23 1773–9, but Regt. No. 20 thereafter; 'Regiment Löwenstein' was the title of Cuirassier Regt. No. 27 1756–8, Dragoon Regt. No. 31 1758–9, and Chevauxleger Regt. No. 18 thereafter. It was not necessary for an *Inhaber* to have had a previous connection with his regiment; Hadik, for example, one of the most famous cavalry commanders, had been colonel of Hussar Regt. Beleznay, but became *Inhaber* of ex-Regt. Ghilányi in 1753, and upon its disbandment in 1768 became *Inhaber* of ex-Regt. Rudolph Pálffy.

Considerable variations in spelling may be encountered in the names of *Inhabers* (and thus of regiments), especially in non-German names. For example, among Hungarian names variations like Nadásd, Nadasdy, Nadasti or Nádasti; and Batthianyi, Batthyány, or Bathiani may be found. Even the names of famous generals may be rendered in several ways (for example Hadik, Haddik, Haddick), and other foreign names may have simple variations like Ayasasa or d'Ayasassa, to phoneticisations like 'Schackmin' for 'Jacquemin'. Occasionally regiments may be found referred to by the name of their commanding officer instead of that of the *Inhaber*.

THE CAVALRY

The cavalry was divided into three basic categories: cuirassiers, the heavy regiments designed for 'shock' action; dragoons, similar but retaining some aspects of their original role as mounted infantry; and hussars, light regiments used initially for skirmishing, raids and reconnaissance. The two former categories were all 'German', and the hussars all Hungarian, formed originally from the indigenous tribesmen of that kingdom and maintaining many of their original attributes. As the period progressed there was a tendency towards 'lightening' the cavalry, resulting in the creation of a new category of 'German' light dragoons, styled chevauxlegers.

Table A: Cavalry regiments *c.* 1769

No. 1 Kaiser-Chevauxlegers	No. 16 Hadik-Huszaren	Mo. 31 St Ignon-Dragoner
No. 2 Kaiser-Huszaren	No. 17 Kálnoky-Huszaren	No. 32 Esterházy-Huszaren
No. 3 Grossherzog von Toscana-Kürassiere	No. 18 Löwenstein-Chevauxlegers	No. 33 Anspach-Kürassiere
No. 4 Erzherzog Maximilian-Kürassiere	No. 19 Hessen-Darmstadt-Dragoner	No. 34 Ujházy-Huszaren
No. 5 Prinz Albert-Carabiniers	No. 20 D'Ayasassa-Kürassiere	No. 35 Bethlén-Huszaren
No. 6 Liechtenstein-Dragoner	No. 21 Trautmannsdorff-Kürassiere	No. 36 Török-Huszaren
No. 7 Batthianyi-Dragoner	No. 22 Kleinhold-Kürassiere	No. 37 Sachsen-Gotha-Dragoner
No. 8 Carl Pálffy-Kürassiere	No. 23 Stampa-Kürassiere	No. 38 Württemberg-Dragoner
No. 9 Savoyen-Dragoner	No. 24 Lusinszky-Huszaren	No. 39 Zweibrücken-Dragoner
No. 10 Modena-Kürassiere	No. 25 Podstatzky-Kürassiere	No. 40 Carlstädter-Grenz-Huszaren
No. 11 Nádasdy-Huszaren	No. 26 Berlichingen-Kürassiere	No. 41 Warasdiner-Grenz-Huszaren
No. 12 Serbelloni-Kürassiere	No. 27 Voghera-Kürassiere	No. 42 Banalisten-Grenz-Huszaren
No. 13 Modena-Dragoner	No. 28 Bettony-Dragoner	No. 43 Slavonier-Grenz-Huszaren
No. 14 O'Donell-Kürassiere	No. 29 Caramelli-Kürassiere	No. 44 Szekler-Huszaren
No. 15 Althann-Kürassiere	No. 30 Nauendorff-Huszaren	No. 45 Wallachisches-Grenz-Dragoner

The system of numbering instituted in 1769 united all categories of cavalry in a single list, including the *Grenz* (frontier) regiments. The numbering of the cavalry regiments changed according to the seniority of the *Inhaber*, but in order to clarify the lineage of the various units, which from changes of *Inhaber* and thus title can be confusing, the 1769 regimental numbers are noted in parentheses after the name of every regiment mentioned in the text (excepting those disbanded before that date), even though the number might not be appropriate for the date at which the unit is mentioned.

Organisation

Organisation was reasonably standard throughout, although there were great fluctuations in strength apart from the usual diminution of numbers caused by the rigours of campaigning; for example, financial restrictions led to reductions even in wartime and, unlike the 'German' regiments, hussar regiments generally maintained a considerably lower establishment in peacetime than their full strength at times of war.

The number of officers and NCOs was considerably fewer than in some armies. Each company was commanded by a captain, styled *Rittmeister* in all cavalry except dragoons, who perpetuated their infantry origin by the use of the infantry rank

Hauptmann or *Hauptleute*. The subalterns were *Lieutenants* ('*Leutnant*' was generally a later spelling) and *Cornets* (*Fähnriche* in the dragoons, in infantry style); these ranks were revised in 1759, *Cornet* and *Fähnriche* being replaced by *Unter-Lieutenant*, and *Lieutenant* by *Ober-Lieutenant*. As field officers nominally retained command of their own companies, from 1748 the actual commander of such a company was styled *Capitän-Lieutenant*. In 1769, when the squadron had replaced the company as the principal tactical element, the captains of each squadron's two companies were ranked in seniority, the squadron-commander becoming the *Premier-Rittmeister* and the commander of the second company the *Seconde-Rittmeister*. The dragoon rank *Hauptleute* was replaced by *Rittmeister* in 1773.

The lowest field rank was *Obrist-Wachtmeister*, titled *Major* from about 1757; the regimental field commander was usually the *Obrist-Lieutenant* (lieutenant-colonel), although there was a colonel commandant (*Obrist*) who conducted regimental affairs in the absence of the *Inhaber*. (The spellings *Obrist* and *Obrist-Lieutenant* were contemporary versions of the more familiar modern German *Oberst* and *Oberst-Leutnant*).

The lowest NCO rank was that of *Corporal* (the contemporary spelling, rather than the more modern *Korporal*), who acted as a platoon-leader. The higher

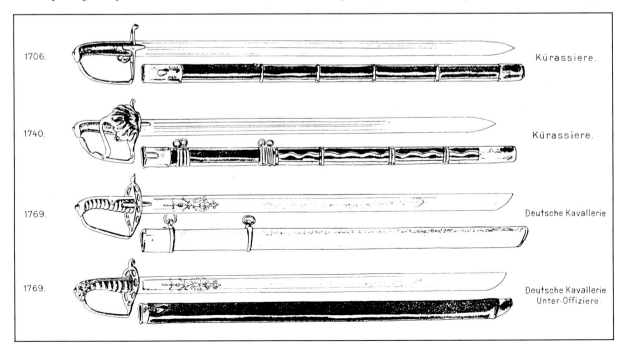

1706.	Kürassiere.
1740.	Kürassiere.
1769.	Deutsche Kavallerie
1769.	Deutsche Kavallerie Unter-Offiziere.

NCO ranks (so-called *Prima Plana*, from their original listing on the first sheet of a unit's muster-roll) were those of *Fourier* (company clerk or quartermaster-corporal) and *Wachtmeister* or sergeant-major; the bearer of the sub-unit's standard was styled the *Estandarten-Führer*. With only one *Wachtmeister* and about three corporals per company, the shortage of NCOs is evident.

At the beginning of the period, each regiment was organised in thirteen companies, one of which was designated as 'élite', carabiniers in the cuirassiers, horse grenadiers in the dragoons. A typical regimental establishment in 1741 was 13 *Wachtmeisters*, 13 *Fouriers*, 13 trumpeters, 12 *Feldschers* (medical orderlies), 26 saddlers and smiths, 40 corporals and 644 troopers. The establishment of 'German' regiments was increased to about 1,000 of all ranks, reduced to about 800 at the end of the War of the Austrian Succession, and considerably fewer for dragoon regiments, as only cuirassiers maintained a full complement of horses in peacetime: the larger horses required by this branch were difficult to acquire, whereas the lighter dragoon mounts could be provided more easily upon mobilisation for war.

Introduced in about 1751, the principal tactical element became the two-company squadron, of which each regiment had six (the élite company remained separate). In 1758 field strength was reduced to five squadrons, the sixth being detached as a reserve, one of its companies acting as a source of replacements for the field squadrons, and the other being used for garrison duty. During the Seven Years' War a typical squadron establishment was ten corporals and 140 men in the 'German' regiments, with one *Rittmeister*, one *Ober-Lieutenant*, one *Unter-Lieutenant* and one *Wachtmeister* per company. After the Seven Years' War establishment varied; the disbanding of some units enabled the others to be made up to one reserve and six field squadrons, and in 1770 regimental organisation was in four divisions of two squadrons, each squadron of 160 men, with a total of 1,303 men per

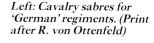

Left: Cavalry sabres for 'German' regiments. (Print after R. von Ottenfeld)

Cuirassier officer with his mount and servant, the latter a trooper wearing the sleeved waistcoat and cloth forage cap. Note the imperial double-eagle device upon the holster-caps. (Print after R. von Ottenfeld)

Left: Heavy cavalry sabre with brass semi-basket hilt, shell-guard and straight blade; an example manufactured before 1740 according to the legend 'Vivat Carlo VI' on the blade of the original.

Right: Heavy cavalry sabre with pipe-backed straight blade and a large, pierced shell-guard, with curved quillons and large, ovoid pommel. The blade-inscription 'Vivat Maria Theresia Regina Hungaria et Bohemia' may indicate a date of c.1742–45, when the army was generally styled 'Royal Bohemian-Hungarian' during the brief period while the Bavarian Charles VII was emperor.

regiment (the balance being the regimental head-quarters personnel). Squadrons were divided into two *Flügel* ('wings'), each of two *Zügen* (platoons).

Hussar regiments were organised similarly, with greatly reduced establishments in peacetime; regimental organisation changed from twelve companies in six squadrons, to ten companies in five squadrons, to seven squadrons, rising to five divisions of two squadrons each by 1781. Typical regimental strength in 1741 was ten *Wachtmeisters*, ten *Fouriers*, seven *Feldschers*, ten trumpeters, ten smiths, ten corporals and 401 men, with squadron-strength rising to 12

corporals and 172 men during the Seven Years' War, with a regimental total at its height of over 1,300 men.

In addition to the regular hussar regiments, a large number of irregulars were mobilised during the War of the Austrian Succession, raised on generally feudal lines, styled *Insurrections-Huszaren*. They were not only largely unorganised but existed upon plunder or whatever gifts their commanders bestowed upon them. From 1751 greater order was imposed, more regiments were created, and they were accorded regular pay and equipment. This tended to reduce the hussars' notoriously predatory nature, but whilst the imposition of greater discipline and order had some tactical benefits, it also diminished the élan enjoyed by the original hussars.

The two types of cavalry both arose from the existing regiments. Created as much to employ the available lighter horses as for tactical reasons, the light dragoons originated in February 1758 when six companies of chevauxlegers were added to Dragoon Regt. Löwenstein (no. 31). In the following March the chevauxleger element was detached and increased to regimental strength as a separate unit, Prince Löwenstein remaining the *Inhaber* (and thus relinquishing proprietorial status of the original dragoon regiment); squadron strength was 12 corporals and 171 men. In February 1760 five dragoon regiments were converted by chevauxlegers, but reverted to dragoons in 1765. Permanent conversions were made from that year, however: Dragoon Regts. Kaiser (no. 1) 1765, Jung-Modena (no. 13) and Hessen-Darmstadt (no. 19) 1773, Kinsky (no. 7) 1775, and Lobkowitz (no. 28) 1779.

The second new branch comprised the two regiments of Carabiniers, created in September 1768 by concentrating the élite companies of the existing cuirassier and dragoon regiments. The 2nd Carabiniers, for example (Regt. Althann, no. 15) was formed from the carabinier companies of Cuirassier Regts. Trautmannsdorff (no. 21), Caramelli (no. 29), de Ville and Pálffy (no. 8), and the grenadiers of Dragoon Regts. Savoyen (no. 9), Liechtenstein (no. 6), Batthianyi (no. 7), Hercules von Modena (no. 13), Darmstadt (no. 19), Bettoni (no. 28), Kolowrat (no. 37), Württemberg (no. 38), Zweibrücken (no. 39) and Althann. Each Carabinier regiment was formed with fourteen companies in seven squadrons, each company comprising one *Rittmeister*, one *Ober-*

Lieutenant, one *Unter-Lieutenant*, one *Fourier*, one *Feldscher*, one musician, one saddler, one smith, one *Wachtmeister*, four corporals and 85 troopers; they continued to be recruited by selecting the best men from the other regiments.

Tactics

The 'German' cavalry manoeuvred by company or squadron, usually marched in column of fours, and formed for action in a three-deep line, the most reliable men on the flanks and in the third rank, and the least impressive in the second rank. In line the subalterns were positioned on the flanks, with the squadron-commander and *Estandarten-Führer* in front; the junior company-commander either rode with them or at the rear of the third line. When the squadron advanced to contact the enemy, the standard-bearer, trumpeter and the centre three files of troopers fell back by some 150 paces, to provide a rallying-point at the conclusion of a charge, to ensure the restoration of order at the earliest opportunity. Advances were delivered at a walk, increasing to a trot about 200 paces before contact with the enemy, and to a gallop only within the last 20 or 30 paces; the speed of attack rarely attained the Prussian-style charge *à outrance*. Except when fighting Turks the use of firearms was discouraged, although carbine-fire (even with fixed bayonets by dragoons) continued to be employed during the Seven Years' War.

Hussars were encouraged to skirmish with fire-arms on the flanks, and at times their manoeuvres were not as rigidly formed as those of the heavier regiments; a Prussian officer described one advance as resembling 'a swarm of bees' and noted that it was especially difficult to estimate the number of hussars in loose formation, especially if no standards could be counted. When firing from the saddle it appears to have been usual to shoot towards the left side, the most natural method to accommodate the butt on the right shoulder; indeed, the Prussian hussar general C.E. von Warnery noted that Austrian hussars at Prague 'fired their carbines at me, which they could easily do, as I was on their left; but their fire, though very near, did not disconcert me, nor did I lose a single man'.

The ability to skirmish with firearms was criticised for potentially discouraging the execution of a more effective attack. One Austrian writer advocated that armour and firearms should be abandoned and all emphasis placed upon rapid and disciplined movement, stating that firing in action only served to provide an excuse for those afraid of charging, that their horses took fright upon the discharge of the carbines. 'It seems inconceivable to me, that for a few uncertain shots ... we should lose the immense advantage of falling on the enemy with the greatest precipitation.' An account supporting this view was given by a Prussian officer who recalled how two battalions marched through a large force of Hungarian cavalry, by forming square with a fieldpiece at each corner and firing whenever the Hungarians came within range: 'It was a pleasure to see how the Hungarians dreaded every cannon-shot, and still more ... the first fire of our front division. From their great superiority in number they seemed very desirous of attacking us; but they could not but perceive

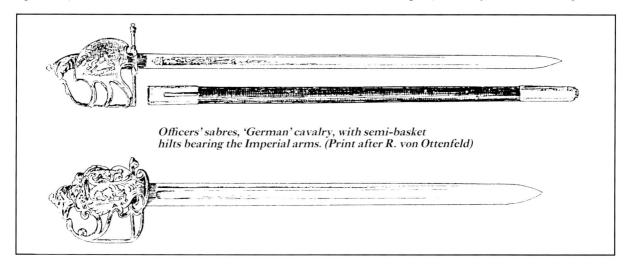

Officers' sabres, 'German' cavalry, with semi-basket hilts bearing the Imperial arms. (Print after R. von Ottenfeld)

that they would not be able to penetrate into so compact a body ... They therefore confined themselves to fire at random with blunderbusses, whereby they wounded some of our men. But their firing we also soon put an end to, by detaching tirailleurs, the distance of 100 paces from our flanks. These side-patroles [*sic*] consisted of 12 men each, who were ordered to keep together, and to support each other by alternate firing.' The officer also recalled that a similar square had been forced to surrender, when the hussars' skirmish-fire had caused such casualties that the square became so choked with dead and wounded that it was unable to move.

The cavalry's reputation suffered during the Seven Years' War, some claiming that their horsemanship and tactical ability, especially that of moving effectively at speed, were inadequate for the duties required. Financial economies from late 1761, which reduced the establishment of 'German' regiments by two squadrons, made them even more unequal to the equivalent Prussian units. Reforms instituted after the Seven Years' War brought a marked improvement; the value of the newer light cavalry was demonstrated during the War of the Bavarian Succession, and from late 1778 the strength of dragoon

and hussar field squadrons was increased to 180 men.

The improvement of discipline and the introduction of regular tactics in the hussars tended to reduce their effectiveness in other ways. The failings of reconnaissance were exemplified by a story concerning Hadik's attempt to capture Torgau in 1758, which was defended by only one Prussian battalion under a Colonel Grollman, plus twenty hussars. Too weak to defend the place, Grollman was determined to bluff the Austrians, so upon their appearance left half his battalion to make the defences appear occupied, and marched out with the remainder, plus the hussars and one fieldpiece. Hadik, believing that so small a force could not possibly intend to meet his vastly superior numbers in the open field, presumed that the advancing Prussian detachment was a ruse to lure him into a trap; the Austrians therefore retreated, an error which would not have occurred had an adequate reconnaissance revealed the weakness of the Prussian position.

A further problem was caused by the lack of a universal hussar uniform, and the similarity between Austrian and Prussian hussar dress. In action it was not difficult to confuse the two sides, and the Prussian Warnery relates an extraordinary incident which occurred during a cavalry action at Prague, fought in a cloud of dust. Having made a charge and seeking to rally his men, Warnery called for a trumpeter to sound the assembly; providentially there was a trumpeter only four yards away, who blew the call. Warnery's Prussians came up, but when the visibility cleared it was discovered that the trumpeter who had sounded the call was, in fact, an Austrian! In 1745 a deliberate subterfuge was perpetrated by the Prussian hussar general Hans Joachim von Zieten, who rode with his regiment through virtually the whole Austrian army, disguising his command by wearing new fur caps and covering their red dolmans with their blue pelisses. Zieten had some Hungarians in his regiment, who spoke that language to any Austrians they encountered, thus completing the illusion that they were an Austrian regiment; their true nationality was only recognised when they were actually through the Austrian forces.

Cuirassiers, 1770. The trumpeter has a red plume, and note the design of the belt worn by the standard-bearer, of facing-coloured cloth with undulating lace in the button-colour. (Print after R. von Ottenfeld)

UNIFORM AND EQUIPMENT

Especially in the early part of the period, considerable latitude was allowed to *Inhabers* regarding the smaller details of uniform and equipment. Some regimental distinctions are noted in the following sections, but they cannot be comprehensive by virtue of space. Some are evident only from contemporary pictures, and it was possible for the minutiae of regimental uniform to be changed with every issue of clothing, which may explain some of the conflicting details that were recorded by various contemporary sources. Some contemporary views of the army, such as those presented in chart form, do not always provide an accurate guide – if illustrations are small or stereotyped they may obscure or fail to distinguish smaller uniform details. Official regulations are similarly not an infallible guide, for in addition to the usual delay between promulgation and implementation of a regulation, in certain cases regulations seem to have been either ignored or adopted only partially; the regulations which specified a blue coat for dragoons in 1757, and a red coat in 1765, for example, seem to have had little effect, as the dragoons' multi-coloured uniforms continued in use. Similarly, an element of circumspection is required with some of the later uniform illustrations, which in some cases conflict with contemporary evidence.

Cuirassiers

Throughout the period the cuirassiers maintained the white coat which was the most characteristic feature of Austrian uniform. This colour may have derived from the buff-leather coat of the 17th century, and indeed two regiments (Anhalt-Zerbst, no. 25, and Anspach, no. 33) briefly resumed using buff-coats in 1762, but they were found unsuitable and a suggestion that they should be generally re-adopted was not pursued. Although red was a universal facing colour (save for Regt. Alt-Modena), there were regimental variations in the arrangement

of buttons and in the colour of waistcoats and breeches. The coat was generally collarless, though Regt. Bretlach (no. 29) had a folding red collar and at least two other regiments had narrow, upright white collars with a collar-patch. The coat was single breasted (in some cases with a row of buttons on each side of the breast), and was worn open to reveal the waistcoat; some illustrations show a strip of facing-coloured cloth fastening together the upper breast, using the top breast-buttons, instead of a conventional collar-patch. The cuffs were of the deep 'gauntlet' pattern with buttons on the upper edge,

Cuirassier field officer, 1770, wearing the coat over the cuirass, which bears the gilded 'dart' on the front, as used by field ranks. (Print after R. von Ottenfeld)

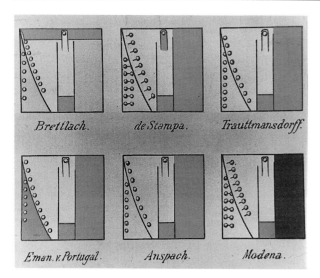

Cuirassier uniform, 1762; shaded sections red for all save Regt. Modena, dark blue, and straw-yellow

waistcoat and breeches for Regt. Bretlach. White buttons save de Stampa and Modena, yellow.

although Morier shows Regt. Diemar (no. 33) *c*. 1748 with a singular, large white cuff-flap. Pockets were horizontal with buttoned flaps, and the skirts were turned back to reveal the lining colour.

The sleeved waistcoat was either single or double breasted, with buttons (or with concealed fastenings for Regt. Anhalt-Zerbst, no. 25), and after the Seven Years' War was generally replaced by a garment made from the cloth of the old coats. Cloth breeches were worn with high-topped boots with interior 'cuffs', although for dismounted duty less cumbersome shoes and stockings were permitted, and for active service ticken overalls with buttons on the outer seam could be worn.

The head-dress was a black tricorn hat with a black bow-shaped cockade and button on the left front. The edges were originally laced in the button-colour, which was removed for all except officers and NCOs from 1758, although it is interesting to note that no hat-lace is depicted in David Morier's paintings of *c*. 1748. A 'secrete' was added inside the hat from 1757, a protective skull-cap made of iron strips. A feature common to all troops was the use of a 'field-sign' (*Feldzeichen*), a sprig of green foliage worn in the head-dress, especially on campaign. Dating from the 17th century, before recognisable uniforms had evolved, this recognition sign was not unique to the Austrian army in the 18th century but

was retained by them longer than in any other army, being used well into the 20th century. Symbols of this kind were also recommended by Frederick the Great, especially for operations at night, 'such as, the turning of the pelisses, wearing the cloaks, or putting a piece of white linen on one arm, a green bough in the cap . . .'; when fighting Austrians who customarily wore their green sprig, the latter could only have been the cause of even greater confusion. 'German' cavalry wore their hair in a long queue, and moustaches were compulsory for enlisted men.

The most characteristic piece of equipment for this branch of the cavalry was the cuirass, an iron breast- and back-plate painted or lacquered black, with a leather or fabric lining and a white leather edging (red edging is shown in later charts). Although Morier shows the back-plate, in an effort to reduce weight it was not generally used. The front-plate was often removed except when action was imminent; even sentries being permitted to perform their duty with their cuirasses laid on the ground. The back-plates were usually held in store to await a campaign against the Turks, when additional protection was deemed necessary. The same applied to 17th-century-style lobster-tailed iron helmets (styled *Pickelhauben*), which were actually issued to the heavy cavalry in 1788–9 for use against the Turks. However, the use of any armour was criticised; one Austrian writer, advocating the lightening of cavalry, remarked that even if the heavy cavalry were 'mounted on dromedaries, barded with plates of steel, twenty hussars who should fall on the flanks of five hundred, might amuse themselves very much at their expence [*sic*] . . . every thing, that is heavy in men and in horses, is useless. Let the arsenals only be decorated with all the cavalry's cuirasses and helmets . . . and be persuaded that a Commander of dragoons, at full speed, will gain a battle. How can you load these poor creatures with so much iron, which only serves to incommode them?'

The *Inhaber* was originally given considerable licence over the pattern of sabre carried by his regiment. The blade was broad and straight, the hilt usually of semi-basket pattern, with scabbards generally constructed of leather over wood, with metallic decoration and reinforcement on the outside. In 1748 blade-length was specified at between 87 and 89 cm, with iron fittings for the rank and file and brass for

NCOs, often gilded or silvered for the higher ranks. (It is sometimes stated that the colour of the metal fittings corresponded with that of the regimental buttons; this is not always confirmed by contemporary pictures.) The semi-basket hilt might include a solid plate, or a shell-shaped guard, which might bear the arms of the *Inhaber*, or later a variation of the monarch's cypher, 'MT' for Maria Theresa, and subsequently 'MTJ' for Maria Theresa and her son. Suspension was from a white leather waist-belt with slings, worn either over or under the skirts of the waistcoat; sword-knots were generally leather for the rank-and-file and woollen for NCOs, but are not always depicted in contemporary pictures. They are shown coloured either white or brown, and from 1769 generally white or yellow for NCOs according to button-colour, sometimes shown with black interweaving.

Equipment included a whitened buff-leather shoulder-belt (sometimes depicted as buff in colour) supporting a smaller version of the infantry cartridge-box with space for fifteen rounds: the box was latterly black, but white boxes are shown in the earlier part of the period (Morier, for example, shows black and white boxes for different regiments at the same date). Another, wider shoulder-belt supported the spring-clip for the carbine, the design of the belt

also varied; Morier, for example, shows one with a large, heart-shaped metal plaque attaching the spring-clip, and earlier illustrations show buff belts with lace decoration, for example yellow lace edging for Regts. Lanthieri (no. 25) and Portugal (no. 26), and red/white/red lace for Regt. Lobkowitz (no. 10). The carbine could also be carried with the butt in a bucket, forward of the right-hand pistol holster. Not until 1750 was a regulated pattern of carbine and pistol introduced; for cuirassiers the carbine used from 1744 was 125 cm long, with a 17 mm bore and no bayonet. From 1759 twelve men in every squadron were equipped with a *Trombon*, a carbine 111 cm long, with an ovoid muzzle akin to that of a blunderbuss, designed to fire buckshot. Other equipment included a water canteen, either drum-shaped or of the characteristically Austrian ovoid construction.

Horse-furniture included a shabraque and holster caps which originally bore the lace, and usually the arms, of the *Inhaber*; Regt. Portugal (no. 26), for example, carried the Portuguese arms on both shabraque and holster-caps. This practice was not universal: in the 1730s, for example, Regt. Caraffa carried 'personal' arms on the shabraque but the cypher of Charles VI on the holster caps. The ground-colour was usually red (some sources show variations),

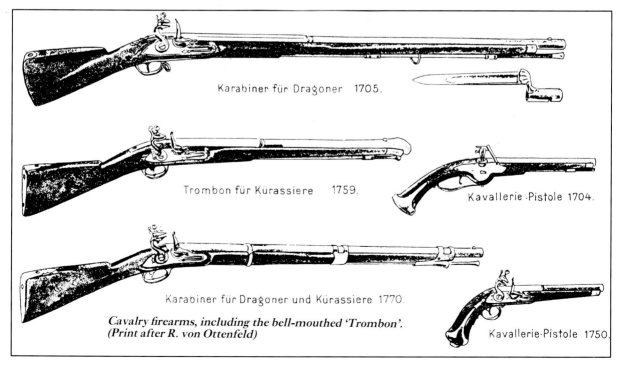

Karabiner für Dragoner 1705.

Trombon für Kürassiere 1759.

Kavallerie-Pistole 1704.

Karabiner für Dragoner und Kürassiere 1770.

Kavallerie-Pistole 1750.

Cavalry firearms, including the bell-mouthed 'Trombon'.
(Print after R. von Ottenfeld)

which was universal from the mid-1750s (less Regt. Alt-Modena, which had dark blue). From about 1754 the arms of the *Inhaber* ceased to be carried, and were replaced by the monarch's cypher (generally in yellow lace with black piping) or double eagle for officers, carried on the rear corners of the shabraque and on the holster caps. The regimental lace was replaced by a universal pattern, depicted with some variations but usually shown as yellow, bearing white diamonds edged blue, with a small blue diamond in the centre of the white. At the rear of the saddle a rolled cloak was carried, usually depicted as white with a red lining visible. Initially it was a large garment, but after the Seven Years' War the cloak was replaced by a *Roquelor*, a sleeved cloak which could be buttoned at the front like a greatcoat.

In 1741 the equipment issued to a cuirassier included the following: every 15 years a cuirass and helmet, the latter held in store for the event of fighting Turks; every ten years a carbine, pair of pistols, carbine belt, cartridge box, sword and belt; every eight years a saddle and harness; every six years a shabraque, holster caps and cloak; every five years a coat; every two and a half years a waistcoat, pair of

breeches, hat and cockade, and pair of boots; and every two years a canvas smock for work. Taking into account that (for example) a carbine and pair of pistols, costing 9 florins together, would last ten years, the annual expense was calculated at 11 florins a man; which for a regiment of 761 other ranks at that date gave a maintenance figure of 8,371 florins per annum.

New facing-colours were introduced in 1765, with yellow buttons for the first named of each of the following pairs of regiments, and white for the second. The colours were: Regts. Erzherzog Leopold (no. 3) and Erzherzog Maximilian (no. 4), poppy-red; Benedikt Daun (no. 27) and Portugal (no. 26), carmine; D'Ayasassa (no. 20) and Kleinhold, pompadour red; Stampach (no. 10) and Serbelloni (no. 12), dark green; Stampa (no. 23) and Anspach (no. 33), parrot-green; Anhalt-Zerbst (no. 25) and Carl Pálffy (no. 8), sea-green; Alt-Modena and Trautmannsdorff (no. 21), dark blue; Prinz Albert (no. 22) and O'Donell (no. 14), light blue; De Ville and Bretlach (no. 29), black.

From 1767 a plume was ordered to be worn by all cavalry. The plume was to be 22 cm high, of black over yellow. In 1769 a single-breasted white coat was introduced, with a very low, upright collar ornamented with a facing-coloured patch (*Paroli*), less voluminous skirts with white turnbacks edged with a broad strip of the facing-colour, and smaller cuffs with two small buttons on the rear seam; pockets were vertical and closed by a single button. Smallclothes were henceforth white or pale straw-yellow, and some regiments are recorded having the front edges of the waistcoat turned back and edged in the facing-colour. In the same year a new sabre was introduced, with an iron knuckle-bow and pierced disc guard, and a wide, straight blade generally between 85 and 87 cm in length. The design was amended slightly in 1773 with the addition of ribs on the backstrap of the hilt, overlapping the leather-covered grip, and by the addition of a pommel-button; the original scabbard of leather over wood was replaced by iron. For

Trooper, Cuirassier Regt. Bentheim (no. 25), painted by David Morier, c. 1748, showing red breeches and a red shabraque with black lace with yellow undulating lines; note the use of the rear plate of the cuirass, normally reserved for actions against the Turks. (The Royal Collection © 1993 Her Majesty the Queen)

Right: 1769-pattern
'German' cavalry sabre
with the 1773 modifications
of the grip-backstrap with
lugs, supporting a bolt
through the grip, and with
the addition of a tang-
button. Iron hilt, ribbed
grip covered with black
leather.

Left: Wachtmeister's
version of the 1769
'German' cavalry sabre,
with a brass hilt including
pierced 'disc' guard and
lion-head pommel;
leather-bound grip,
straight blade.

colour. The universal symbol of commissioned rank in the Austrian army was the waist-sash (*Feldbinde*) of gold with black interweaving (the colours of the imperial arms), with knot and tassels of the same colours. Charles VII of Bavaria (1743–5), changed the sash to grass-green with gold and silver interweaving. With the reintroduction of the gold and black pattern, gold lace was restricted to general officers, with yellow and black silk for field ranks and camelhair for others; this was reflected in the cost, which in 1748 was 40 florins for a sash of field officers, 20 for the captains' version, and 15 for subalterns. Sword-knots were also of metallic lace, with spangles for field ranks. Officers' cuirasses had gilt studs and shoulder-straps and red cloth lining, and often a decorative gilt 'wedge' on the front, increased in size with rank, extending up to half-way down the breast for subalterns and to the bottom edge for higher ranks, though this is not always depicted. Officers' sabres had gilded mounts, semi-basket hilts – often bearing the imperial arms – and black leather scabbards. Latterly officers could wear a full-skirted coat in the regimental colouring over the cuirass.

Wachtmeisters and standard-bearers usually had gold hat-lace and corporals silver, although it is sometimes stated that the colouring might match that of the regimental buttons. A further distinctive symbol of NCO rank was the cane, of 'Spanish reed' for *Wachtmeisters* and hazel for corporals. Rank distinctions were also carried on the shabraque: for the rank and file the lace edging was one and a half inches wide, with a double row for corporals, one wide and one narrow band for carabiniers, and three lines for *Wachtmeisters* and standard-bearers. Officers' shabraques were edged with gold lace, for field ranks with two two-inch laces and fringe, *Rittmeisters* the same without fringe, for subalterns a one-inch lace, and for *capitän-lieutenants* one broad and one narrow.

In the earlier years the dress of musicians was probably dependent upon the taste of the *Inhaber*, so a number of variously coloured uniforms are indicated; but after about 1755 they appear to have worn ordinary uniform, sometimes shown with 'swallows'-nest' wings, and for cuirassier musicians always without the cuirass. Later on, red or the ordinary black and yellow plumes are recorded; musicians were armed with sabres and pistols, but not carbines.

Wachtmeisters the hilt often had a lion-head pommel, with metalwork brass or gilded; a variation of the scabbard was covered in brown leather, with suspension by means of a frog-stud instead of the ordinary slings. A new carbine was introduced in 1770, with iron mounts and no bayonet, 123 cm long and with a new calibre of 18.3 mm; a pistol with matching calibre was introduced at the same time.

Officers' uniforms were like those of the other ranks, but of finer quality; their hats had a metallic lace border, and their waistcoats had a double row of lace for field ranks and single for subalterns. The lace is usually recorded as gold, but earlier examples are recorded in silver, for regiments with that button-

Grenadier, Dragoon Regt. Batthianyi (no. 7), painted by David Morier c. 1748, wearing a blue coat with scarlet facings, waistcoat, breeches and aiguillette. This gives an excellent view of the rear of the grenadier cap; the bag is scarlet with yellow or gold lace edging and tassel. The red shabraque has yellow lace with black stripes. (The Royal Collection © 1993 Her Majesty the Queen)

Dragoons

Uniform and equipment of the dragoons was in many respects similar to that of cuirassiers, though with a number of marked differences, and no issue of cuirass or helmets.

Dragoon coats came in a variety of colours, with contrasting facings. Most had lapels, usually depicted as having buttons in groups of three, plus a single button at the top of each lapel; a further distinction was the aiguillette worn at the rear of the right shoulder. Smallclothes and hats were similar to those of cuirassiers, but the dragoon grenadiers wore the infantry-style black bearskin grenadier cap, with a coloured bag hanging at the rear, trimmed with lace and tassel, and often with a front-plate. The design of cap varied: prior to the accession of Maria Theresa, for example, Regt. Savoyen (no. 9) wore a cap with a large gilt plate bearing the cross of Savoy as its main symbol; Regt. Batthianyi (no. 7) had a plate with a rounded top, a brass edge and bearing a brass grenade upon a red ground; Regt. Khevenhuller (no. 13) wore a mitre cap instead of a bearskin, the front bearing a crowned shield inscribed with Charles VI's cypher over a grenade; Regt. Ligne (no. 31) wore a cap with no plate, a style also shown by Morier for Regt. Liechtenstein (no. 6).

Equipment was similar to that of cuirassiers, with broader belts for the horse grenadiers (as for carabiniers) and larger cartridge boxes for the élite companies. There were considerable regimental differences, especially in the early part of the period: for example, on their buff-leather belts Regt. Batthianyi (no. 7) is shown with a black pouch bearing a central brass badge of a crowned escutcheon; Savoyen (no. 9) a black pouch bearing a large brass badge in the centre, inscribed with the cross of Savoy, with separate grenade-badges in the lower corners; Khevenhuller (no. 13) a buff pouch bearing a crowned shield inscribed with the cypher of Charles VI, with separate grenades in the lower corners; and Ligne (no. 31) a black pouch bearing a circular brass plate. Morier shows predominantly black pouches but buff-leather, with no badge, for Regt. Styrum. Brass match-cases were usually worn on the front of the grenadiers' belts, but this is not present in Morier's depiction of Regt. Batthianyi (no. 7).

There was apparently greater variation in the pattern of sabre carried by dragoons; Morier shows curved sabres carried by some, including Regt. Batthianyi. Prior to the adoption of the 1769 sabre, leather-covered scabbards are usually shown, with suspension from a waist belt frog instead of the slings used by cuirassiers. The 1744 dragoon carbine had iron mounts and a bayonet, was 125 cm in length and had a 17 mm bore. Bayonets were withdrawn in 1769, but in addition to the 1770 carbine as carried by cuirassiers, dragoons and chevauxlegers received the remarkable Crespi carbine from that year. Designed by a Milanese clockmaker, Giuseppe Crespi, it was a breech-loading weapon of considerable ingenuity, and was copied in Britain by the gunmaker Durs Egg in the late 1780s, resulting in an abortive trial for use by the British Army. Austria persevered longer with the breech-loader, but the imperfect seal between barrel and opening breech made it dangerous to fire, and after many men were burned during the War of the Bavarian Succession, it was withdrawn in 1779. Its bayonet was a curious spear on the end of a rod, and when 'unfixed' was carried under the barrel, with the spear blade within a socket forward of the trigger guard. The Crespi was of the same length and calibre as the ordinary carbine. Another unusual weapon issued to a few men in each dragoon grenadier company was the grenade-projector, a bell-mouthed weapon styled a *Musqueton-Granatepistole* or *Gewehrhaubitze*.

Although in many respects dragoon equipment and rank distinction were like those of cuirassiers, they perpetuated their mounted-infantry origin by having drummers with infantry-style drums. As with the trumpeters mentioned above, by the mid-1750s distinctively coloured uniforms seem to have been replaced by ordinary dress with the addition of 'swallows'-nest' wings with lace decoration; drummers were armed only with swords. Dragoon horse-furniture was similar to that of cuirassiers, but prior to the adoption of the universal pattern of housings, there appears to have been less use of *Inhabers'* arms on shabraque and holster caps, decoration often being limited to regimentally coloured lace; for example, plain horse-furniture is shown for Regts. Batthianyi (no. 7), Liechtenstein (no. 6), Khevenhuller (no. 13) and Ligne (no. 31), among others.

In 1757 it was intended to introduce dark blue as the ground-colour for all dragoon uniforms, but the order seems to have had little effect and the multi-coloured coats remained in use. (Such a profound change in uniform colour could have been hazardous on service, if replacements wore the new uniform while others retained their old style, which might result in confusion and a somewhat piebald appearance, as happened with Regt. Ligne (no. 31) in mid-1757.) In 1765 new regulations specified a red coat for all regiments, with the following facings, and white buttons for the first-named of each of the following pairs of regiments, and yellow for the second:

Regts. Römischer König (or Kaiser) (no. 1) and Darmstadt (no. 19), dark green; Kolowrat (no. 37) and Zweibrücken (no. 39), parrot-green; Württemberg (no. 38) and Savoyen (no. 9), black; Sachsen-Gotha (no. 28) and Batthianyi (no. 7), light blue; Jung-Modena (no. 13) and Liechtenstein (no. 6), dark blue; and for Regt. Althann sea-green or lemon-yellow facings and yellow or white buttons.

In 1767, however, a white single-breasted coat was specified, with a folding collar, cuffs and edging to the white turnbacks in the facing-colour. Facings were as follows (with 1769 numbers): nos. 6 and 28, light blue; 7 and 13, dark blue; 9 and 38, black; 19, dark green; 31 and 37, red; and 39 and Regt. Althann, sea-green; with white buttons for nos. 13, 28, 37, 38 and Althann, and yellow for the remainder. Some sources show no aiguillettes with this uniform, whilst

Dragoon drummer, showing a laced hat and the use of patterned lace on the wings. (Print after R. von Ottenfeld)

The Crespi breech-loading carbine, with spear-headed 'rod'-bayonet, showing the mode of carrying it below the barrel when 'unfixed'. (Print after R. von Ottenfeld)

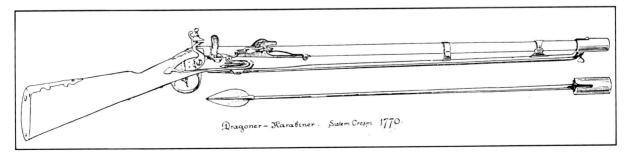

Dragoner - Karabiner. Sistem Crespi 1770.

others indicate a universal yellow aiguillette. Some illustrations show the coat worn unfastened, with the waist belt which supported the sword worn over the waistcoat but under the coat. The 1769 sabre was worn with slings from the waist belt, whereas the earlier patterns had usually (but not invariably) been suspended from frogs.

Chevauxlegers

Chevauxleger equipment was mostly like that of the dragoons, and indeed the temporary conversion of some regiments involved no amendment to the basic uniform. The first regiment, Löwenstein (no. 18), from 1759 wore a grass green coat with red facings, waistcoat and breeches and yellow buttons, and a head-dress of a black felt, false-fronted and peakless

Casquet, the front 23 cm high and the rear 16 cm, with yellow edging, a brass plate bearing the monarch's cypher, and a yellow and black pompon at the left. This colour-scheme was retained, latterly with a green waistcoat and white breeches, and was also specified in 1765 for the converted St. Ignon regiment, with white buttons. Officers wore bicorns, and trumpeters had 'reversed colours'. The *Casquet* was worn with the white 1767 dragoon uniform by regiments nominated as Chevauxlegers, other than those wearing green.

Hussars

The elaborate hussar uniform was inspired by the national dress of the Hungarian tribesmen who originally formed the hussar corps. The head-dress

Grenadier, Dragoon Regt. Ligne (no. 31), painted by David Morier c. 1748, in a uniform ascribed to this corps despite it being blue instead of the regiment's more familiar green. Blue waistcoat and breeches, red facings and aiguillette, red cap-bag with gold or yellow lace and tassel, red cap-plate with brass edge and grenade. The buff belts have an undulating line of decorative stitching down the middle, a feature shown in other Morier paintings; note also the brown wooden canteen, the iron-shod picket-stake and the tuft of red fabric stuck into the carbine-muzzle to exclude moisture. (The Royal Collection © 1993 Her Majesty the Queen)

was a fur busby or *Kalpak*, with a hanging cloth bag, a development from a stocking-cap with fur head-band, a style depicted in use as late as the mid 1730s. The busby was sometimes replaced by a tall, felt cap; Morier shows one with an unfolded 'wing' like a mirliton cap. The jacket was a braided, tailless dolman, worn with a fur-edged, braided pelisse which could be worn as a jacket or slung over the shoulder. Originally the hussars appear to have worn leather breeches under thigh-length, coloured cloth leggings (*Scharawaden*), but these seem to have declined in use by the Seven Years' War, and coloured breeches worn instead (both styles are shown by Morier in the late 1740s); the boots were of the distinctive Hungarian style. The waist-sash had contrastingly coloured 'barrels', of which a number of styles are depicted, some with the barrels arranged in blocks, some scattered at random, and others with a coloured bar or 'knot' at the front of a solidly coloured sash.

Some equipment resembled that of the 'German' cavalry, but the sabre was usually suspended on slings from a narrow waist belt, as was the sabretache, the face of which was decorated according to the choice of the *Inhaber*. The sabre was a version of the Hungarian 'native' weapon, with a curved blade and stirrup hilt, the design originally left to the *Inhaber*. Scabbard-decoration was varied, originally similar to the style used by 'German' regiments. From 1768 a blade-length of 84 cm was specified, with an iron stirrup hilt and iron scabbard for troopers, and a black leather scabbard with iron mounts for corporals; for *Wachtmeisters* the scabbard was of black

Chevauxleger (left) and hussar, c. 1778; the hussar has a waterproof cover over his plume, wears the pelisse as a jacket, and carries his sabre ready for action suspended by the sword-knot from his wrist. (Print after R. von Ottenfeld)

Trooper, Hussar Regt. Kálnoky (no. 17), painted by David Morier, c. 1748; dark blue dolman, pelisse, busby-bag and scharawaden *(worn over buff breeches), yellow braid, red boots, red sash with blue barrels, buff belts, dark blue shabraque with yellow decoration, including the* Inhaber's *arms, and white cloak over the front of the saddle. The fringed harness is a feature of most of Morier's paintings of hussars; and note the buff leather reinforcing on the elbows and side-seams of the dolman. (The Royal Collection © 1993 Her Majesty the Queen)*

leather, with brass or gilded fittings and hilt. Hussar carbines were short, the brass-mounted 1744 weapon having a length of 90 cm and a bore of 17 mm; the iron-mounted 1770 pattern was the same length but with a bore of 18.3 mm, reverting again to 17 mm in 1779. In addition to their unique uniform and equipment, the hussars had a distinctive hairstyle, the hair at the temples braided and hanging in plaits, with moustaches worn by all.

Horse-furniture included a 'Hungarian' saddle and pointed-ended shabraque which often had elaborate embroidered decoration, including the *Inhaber*'s arms. As for the 'German' cavalry, a universal pattern of shabraque was introduced, in red with mixed yellow and black braid, bearing the monarch's cypher in the rear corners.

Contemporary pictures show a wide variety of styles and colouring, particularly in the minutiae of hussar uniform, and some contemporary illustrations suggest that later reconstructions of hussar uniform tend to over-simplify the design of braid. The uniform of the oldest hussar regiment, Nádasdy (no. 11), exemplifies the change of uniform-colour and the conflicting information which has been recorded (see below).

Elements of 'German'-style uniform were worn

1: Trooper, Cuirassier Regt. Diemar, 1748
2: Trooper, Cuirassier Regt. De Ville
3: Cuirassier officer

WRy. 93

A

1: Trooper, Cuirassier Regt. Alt-Modena
2: NCO, Cuirassier Regt. Bretlach
3: Trooper, Cuirassier Regt. Anhalt-Zerbst

WRV. 93

B

1: Grenadier, Dragoon Regt. Liechtenstein, 1748
2: Grenadier, Dragoon Regt. Batthianyi
3: Trooper, Dragoon Regt. Sachsen-Gotha

WRJ. 93

1: Officer, Dragoon Regt. 'Savoyen'
2: Drummer, Dragoon Regt. Löwenstein, c.1758
3: Trooper, Dragoon Regt. Hessen-Darmstadt
4: Trooper, Dragoon Regt. Althann

WRy. 93

D

1: Trooper, Hussar Regt. Károlyi, c.1748
2: Trooper, Hussar Regt. P.A. Esterhazy
3: Trooper, Hussar Regt. Kaiser

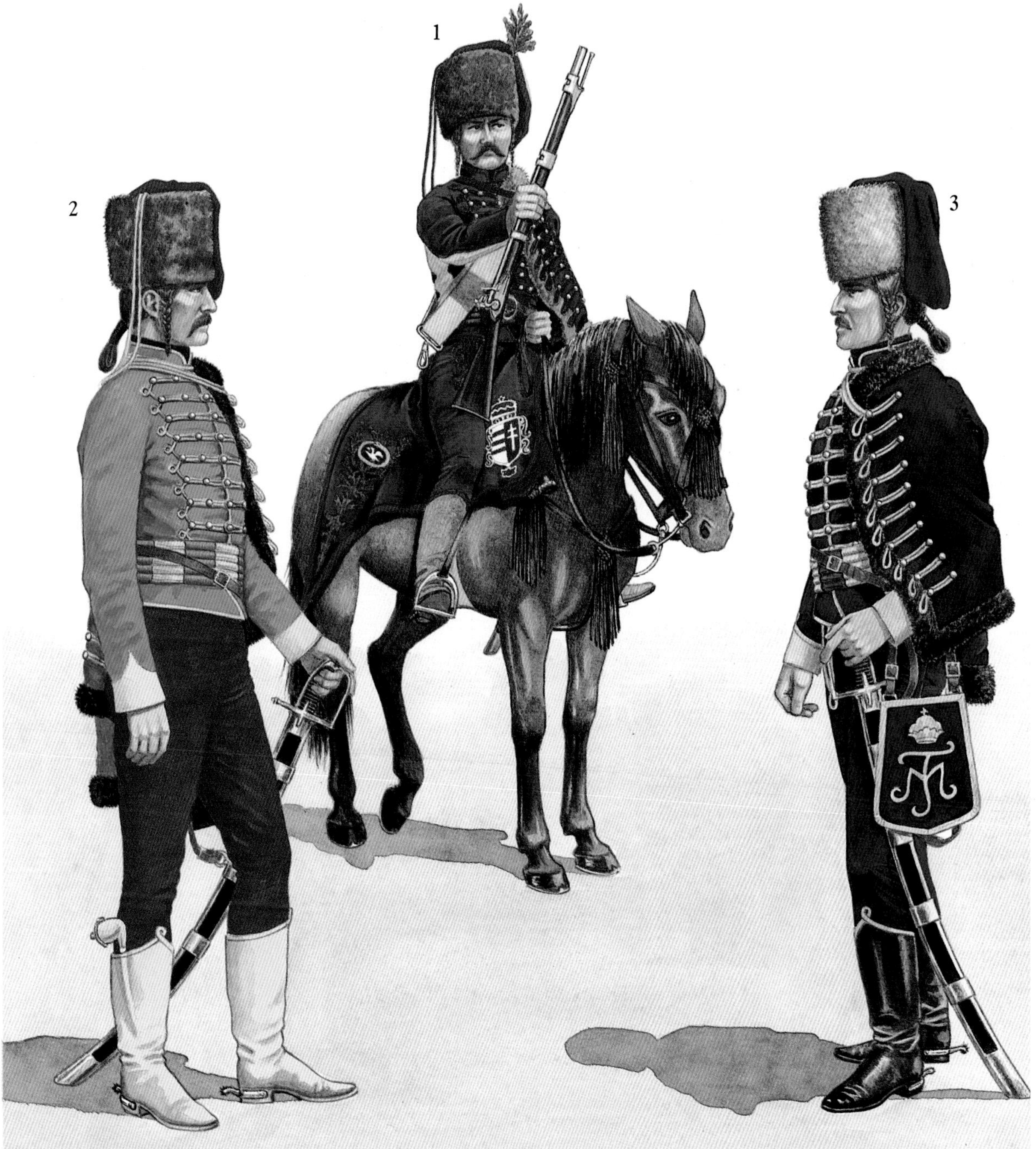
1
2
3
WR/93

E

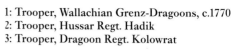

1: Trooper, Wallachian Grenz-Dragoons, c.1770
2: Trooper, Hussar Regt. Hadik
3: Trooper, Dragoon Regt. Kolowrat

F

1: Trooper, Hussar Regt. Kálnoky, 1772
2: Officer, Palatinal Hussars
3: Trooper, Hussar Regt. Baranyay

WR. 93

1: Trooper, Chevauxleger Regt. Löwenstein, c.1770
2: Trooper, Dragoon Regt. 'Savoyen', c.1775
3: NCO Trumpeter, Cuirassier Regt. Caramelli, 1770

WRY. 93

by some hussars. Trumpeters wore a laced bicorn and German-style coat with Hungarian-style braiding, worn over a waistcoat braided in dolman-style; some gaudily coloured coats are recorded, such as red with gold lace worn by trumpeters of Regt. Paul Esterházy (no. 24), or light yellow with silver lace by Regt. Kálnoky (no. 17). *Fouriers* wore bicorns with gold or silver lace edging, and a coat of the pelisse-colour over a waistcoat of the dolman-colour. Officers' uniforms were generally like those of the other ranks, but in finer material and with silver or gold lace; although for undress they also had a more 'German' uniform, including a laced tricorn, white frock-coat with Hungarian-style braid, a dolman-coloured braided waistcoat and ordinary legwear. NCOs were generally distinguished by design of sword-knot, as with the 'German' cavalry, and there is also evidence for their use of metallic lace; for Regt. Károlyi (no. 16), for example, there is mention of gold and silver braid on the dolman, and gold lace on sabretache and pouch.

An attempt to introduce dark blue uniforms in 1757 had no effect, but new uniforms were decreed in 1767. These imposed a single colour for dolman, pelisse and breeches, as follows (using 1769 numbers): Regts. 2, 24, 32 and Hadik, dark blue; 16, 17, 35 and 36, light blue; 11 and E. Esterházy, dark green;

and 30 and 34, parrot-green. Buttons were white for Regts. 34, 36 and E. Esterházy, and yellow for the remainder. Sabretaches and rank and file lace were yellow for Regts. 2 and 16, crimson for 11, 17 and 32, red for 24, 30 and 35, white for 34, 36 and E. Esterházy, and orange for Hadik with the following exceptions of sabretache-colour: Regt. 2 dark blue, 16 and 36 light blue; E. Esterházy dark green. However, a universal mixed black and yellow lace was adopted, and red sabretaches with this braid and bearing the monarch's cypher, matching the colouring and decoration of the shabraque. The hussar boots had a black and yellow braid edge and rosette; NCOs had yellow lace.

Although officers and *Wachtmeisters* retained their busbies, the ordinary head-dress became a peakless, felt *Czakelhaube* (shako) with a black and yellow rosette and pompon on the front and similarly coloured cords. For the ten regular regiments in 1772, when the issue of felt caps seems to have been completed, the colour of the *Czakelhaube* was black for Regts. 2, 11, 16 and 30; grey for 32 and 36, green for 24 and 35, red for 17 and light blue for 34. The four Grenz (border) hussar regiments (nos. 40–43) had grass green dolman and pelisse (43 parrot green), red dolman-cuffs and breeches, yellow braid and sashes and black shakos.

An early hussar uniform, showing the origins of the later style, including a stocking-cap with fur head-band which evolved into the busby. The sabre with quillons but no knuckle-bow was probably the most common style prior to about 1740. (Print after R. von Ottenfeld)

REGIMENTAL DETAILS

The following includes some of the principal features of regimental uniform, but these details cannot be comprehensive and refer mainly to the period prior to the post-Seven Years' War uniform-change, detailed above. The place of recruitment was within the empire unless otherwise specified; regiments disbanded before the allocation of 1769 numbers are referred to by the name of the *Inhaber* at the beginning of the period, unless this could be confused with another regiment, in which case the name of a subsequent *Inhaber* is used.

Cuirassiers

Note: 'facings' refers to colouring of cuffs, turnbacks and shoulder-straps unless otherwise specified; and a single row of buttons on coat and waistcoat unless otherwise specified.

Cuirassier Regt. No. 3

Titles: 1740 Hohenzollern-Hechingen, 1750 Erzherzog Leopold; from 1765, when Leopold succeeded his father Francis Stephen as grand duke of Tuscany, an alternative designation was 'Grossherzog von Toscana'. Converted to dragoons 1775.

Uniform: red facings and breeches (Ottenfeld indicates white shoulder-straps), white waistcoat and buttons. After

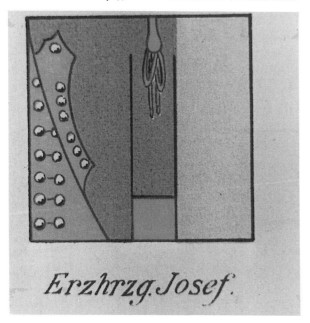

Erzhrzg. Josef.

conversion to dragoons the uniform remained white with red facings, the cuirassier-style coat having a red collar-patch, and a white waistcoat with turned-back front corners laced red.

Cuirassier Regt. No. 4

Titles: 1740 Hohenembs, 1756 Erzherzog Ferdinand, 1761 Erzherzog Maximilian. Originally a Florentine corps which entered Habsburg service in 1619; recruited in the 'Hereditary Lands' (*Erblanden*).

Uniform: red facings and breeches, white waistcoat and shoulder-strap, yellow buttons (indicated either in threes or spaced singly on the coat).

Cuirassier Regt. No. 8

Titles: 1740 Carl Pálffy, 1774 Rothschütz.

Uniform: red facings and breeches, white shoulder-strap (Ottenfeld indicates red), white waistcoat and buttons.

Cuirassier Regt. No. 10

Titles: 1740 Lobkowitz, 1753 Stampach, 1768 Modena (not to be confused with Regt. Alt-Modena which had blue facings).

Uniform: red facings and waistcoat (Ottenfeld indicates white shoulder-strap), straw-yellow breeches (Knötel shows red), yellow buttons (double row on coat and waistcoat).

Cuirassier Regt. No. 12

Titles: 1740 Seherr, 1743 Saint-Ignon, 1745 Serbelloni, 1778 Mecklenburg-Strelitz.

Uniform: red facings, waistcoat and breeches, white shoulder-straps (Ottenfeld indicates red), white buttons (double row on coat and waistcoat; Ottenfeld indicates yellow, with single row on waistcoat).

Cuirassier Regt. No. 14

Titles: 1740 Cordua, 1756 O'Donell (common spelling: *Inhaber* was the noted cavalry general whose name is also spelled 'O'Donnell'), 1773 Brockhausen, 1779 Haag. Recruited in the Empire and Netherlands.

Uniform: red facings and breeches (Ottenfeld indicates white shoulder-strap), white waistcoat, yellow buttons (Ottenfeld indicates in threes on coat). The Albertini MS (1762) shows a low white collar with red patch.

Cuirassier Regt. No. 20

Titles: 1740 Miglio, 1745 Schmerzing, 1762 D'Ayasassa, 1779 Jacquemin. Recruited in Bohemia.

Uniform, Regt. Erzherzog Joseph, 1762; green coat, red facings, waistcoat and aiguillette, straw-yellow breeches, yellow buttons.

Uniform: red facings and breeches, white waistcoat, yellow buttons (double row on coat and waistcoat; Ottenfeld indicates white shoulder-strap and single row of buttons on waistcoat).

Cuirassier Regt. No. 21
Titles: 1740 Bernes, 1751 Trautmannsdorff.
Uniform: red facings and breeches, white waistcoat and buttons; Ottenfeld and Knötel show white shoulder-straps.

Cuirassier Regt. No. 22
Titles: 1740 Saint-Ignon, 1750 Kalckreuth, 1760 Prinz Albert (of Saxe-Teschen; 'Sachsen-Teschen' was an alternative regimental designation), 1768 Kleinhold (or Kleinholdt), 1773 Thurn. Disbanded 1775.
Uniform: red facings and waistcoat, straw-yellow breeches, low white collar, yellow buttons; Ottenfeld indicates white shoulder-strap, coat-buttons in threes.

Cuirassier Regt. No. 23
Titles: 1740 Birkenfeld, 1761 Stampa (or de Stampa), 1773 Jacquemin. Third oldest of the cavalry regiments, formed 1636; disbanded 1775.
Uniform: red facings and breeches, white waistcoat, yellow buttons (double row on waistcoat).

Cuirassier Regt. No. 25
Titles: 1740 Lanthieri, 1745 Bentheim, 1751 Stampach, 1753 Anhalt-Zerbst (alternatively 'Zerbst'), 1767 Podstatzky. Recruited in Bohemia; disbanded 1775.
Uniform: see Plate B3.

Cuirassier Regt. No. 26
Titles: 1740 Portugal (*Inhaber* was Don Emmanuel of Portugal; the family connection arose from the marriage in 1708 of King John V of Portugal (1689–1750) to Maria Anna, daughter of the Emperor Leopold I), 1766 Berlichingen. Recruited in Bohemia; converted to dragoons 1779.
Uniform: red facings, waistcoat and breeches, white buttons; Ottenfeld indicates a white shoulder-strap.

Cuirassier Regt. No. 27
Titles: 1740 Johann Pálffy, 1751 Radicati, 1756 Löwenstein (or Löwenstein-Wertheim), 1758 Benedikt Daun (not to be confused with Field-Marshal Leopold Daun), 1766 Voghera. Recruited in the Empire and Bohemia.
Uniform: red facings and breeches, white shoulder-straps and waistcoat, yellow buttons, double row on waistcoat (Ottenfeld indicates a red folding collar, buttons in threes on coat and single row on waistcoat).

Cuirassier Regt. No. 29
Titles: 1740 Lubomirski, 1745 Bretlach (also 'Bretlack', 'Brettlach' or 'Pretlach'), 1767 Caramelli.
Uniform: see Plate B2.

Cuirassier Regt. No. 33
Titles: 1740 Diemar, 1751 Anspach (alternatively Anspach-Bayreuth; the margrave of that state was *Inhaber*).
Uniform: red facings and breeches, white shoulder-straps, waistcoat and buttons (two rows on waistcoat, though Ottenfeld indicates one).

Hungarian cavalry in combat, an illustration which conveys the somewhat wild nature of these troops. (Print after Adolph Menzel)

Cuirassier Regt. De Ville

Titles: 1740 Berlichingen, 1751 Gelhay, 1759 De Ville (or 'Ville'). Recruited in Bohemia, disbanded 1768.
Uniform: See Plate A2.

Cuirassier Regt. Caraffa

Titles: 1740 Caraffa, 1743 Lucchesi (or Lucchesi d'Abarra), 1758 Buccow, 1764 Kleinhold (or Kleinholdt). Recruited in Westphalia, disbanded 1768.
Uniform: red facings, breeches and waistcoat, white buttons (two rows on waistcoat; Ottenfeld shows one row, white shoulder-straps, buttons in threes on coat).

Cuirassier Regt. Alt-Modena

Titles: 1740 Podstatzky, 1743 Czernin, 1755 Alt-Modena (titled thus to distinguish it from Dragoon Regt. No. 13, which from 1756 was titled Jung-Modena; the *Inhaber* was the Duke of Modena, Francesco D'Este, who from 1753 was governor and commander of the Austrian troops in Lombardy. Recruited in Lombardy, disbanded 1768.
Uniform: See Plate B1.

Dragoons

Note: 'facings' refers to colour of cuffs, lapels, turnbacks, shoulder-straps and aiguillettes, unless otherwise specified; and a single row of buttons on the waistcoat unless otherwise specified.

Dragoon Regt. No. 1

Titles: 1740 Althann, 1748 Erzherzog Joseph (from 1765 his position as emperor gave the corps the title Kaiser; also Römischer König). Converted to Chevauxlegers 1765.
Uniform: green coat and waistcoat, red facings, yellow buttons (double row on waistcoat), straw-yellow breeches; Ottenfeld indicates red waistcoat. As Chevauxlegers, grass green coat with poppy-red facings, white breeches.

Dragoon Regt. No. 6

Title: Liechtenstein. Disbanded 1775.
Uniform: See Plate C1.

Dragoon Regt. No. 7

Titles: 1740 Bathianyi (or Batthyány), 1773 Kinsky. Second oldest of the cavalry regiments, and oldest of the dragoons, formed 1631; converted to Chevauxlegers 1775.
Uniform: see Plate C2.

Dragoon Regt. No. 9

Titles: 1740 Aspremont-Linden, 1773 Richecour. Despite the names of these *Inhabers*, the regimental connection with Prince Eugene of Savoy was so strong that the regiment was generally styled 'Savoyen'.
Uniform: see Plate D1.

Dragoon Regt. No. 13

Titles: 1740 Khevenhüller, 1744 Holly, 1756 Jung-Modena (*Inhaber* was the Erbprinz of Modena; also styled 'Hercules von Modena'). Recruited in Bohemia and the Empire; converted to Chevauxlegers 1773.
Uniform: red coat and shoulder-strap, light blue facings and breeches, light blue low collar shown 1762 but not indicated by Ottenfeld, white aiguillette (Ottenfeld light blue), white buttons (double row on waistcoat; Ottenfeld indicates yellow, single row).

Dragoon Regt. No. 19

Titles: 1740 D'Ollone, 1746 Hessen-Darmstadt (*Inhaber* was originally Louis VIII, landgrave of that state, which was loyal to Austria, although his successor, Louis IX, served under Frederick the Great). Converted to Chevauxlegers 1773.
Uniform: see Plate D3.

Dragoon Regt. No. 28

Titles: 1740 Sachsen-Gotha, 1767 Bettony (or Bettoni), 1773 Lobkowitz. Recruited in southern Germany; con-

Dragoons c. 1756; the grenadier (left) in this print after R. von Ottenfeld has the undulating lace on the cap-bag which is not shown by some contemporary sources.

verted to Chevauxlegers in 1760 and again in 1779.
Uniform: see Plate C3.

Dragoon Regt. No. 31
Titles: 1740 Ligne, 1757 Benedikt Daun, 1758 Löwenstein, 1759 Saint-Ignon, 1779 D'Arberg. Recruited in the Netherlands; one of the most famous regiments in the army, performing a legendary charge at Kolin. Converted to Chevauxlegers 1760, but back to dragoons 1765.
Uniform: see Plate D2.

Dragoon Regt. No. 37
Titles: 1740 Römer, 1741 Philibert, 1753 Kolowrat (or Kollowrat, or Kollowrat-Krakowsky), 1769 Sachsen-Gotha. Recruited in Lower Austria and Bohemia. The regiment's service at Mollwitz provides an example of a unit acting in battle under the command of its *Inhaber*, not a common occurrence: it participated in the charge of Lt.Gen. Carl Römer against the Prussian right wing, during which Römer was killed.
Uniform: see Plate F3.

Dragoon Regt. No. 38
Title: Württemberg. The *Inhaber*, Charles Eugene, Duke of Württemberg (1728–93), did not come of age until 1744. His father, Duke Charles Alexander, had been an officer in Austrian service, and converted to Roman Catholicism; Charles Eugene made himself unpopular with his largely Protestant subjects by fighting against Prussia in the Seven Years' War.
Uniform: red coat and shoulder strap, black facings, light straw breeches and waistcoat, yellow buttons (Ottenfeld shows white buttons, two rows on waistcoat).

Dragoon Regt. No. 39
Title: Zweibrücken. This small territory was a state in the Palatinate, known as Deux-Ponts in French; its ruling family provided not only the *Inhaber* of this regiment, but under the title 'Duc des Deux-Ponts' also held the colonelcy of the *Régiment Deux-Ponts* in the French army.
Uniform: dark blue coat and waistcoat, red facings, light straw breeches, yellow buttons; Ottenfeld indicates red waistcoat.

Dragoon Regt. No. 45
Title: Wallachisches-Grenz-Dragoner-Regiment. A regi-

ment of *Grenz* (border) cavalry, raised in Transylvania 1763, disbanded 1771.
Uniform: see Plate F1.

Dragoon Regt. Limburg-Styrum
Title: Limburg-Styrum; disbanded 1748.
Uniform: red coat with green facings (although Morier shows blue or bluish facings and aiguillette), white buttons, straw-yellow breeches.

Dragoon Regt. Preysing
Title: Preysing; disbanded 1750.
Uniform: red coat with blue facings.

Dragoon Regt. Koháry
Titles: 1740 Koháry, 1758 Althann. Disbanded 1768.
Uniform: see Plate D4.

Staff Dragoons
The *Stabs-Dragoner-Regiment* was formed 1758 to perform staff and escort duty; disbanded at the conclusion of the Seven Years' War but re-formed in 1769.
Uniform: dark blue coat and waistcoat, red cuffs, shoulder-strap, breeches, white turnbacks and aiguillette, yellow buttons, no lapels; also recorded with light straw breeches and a red 'collar'-patch by the upper coat-buttons.

Chevauxleger Regt. No. 18
Title: 1759 Jung-Löwenstein or Löwenstein-Wertheim.

Dragoon grenadier, wearing the grenadier cap with a line of undulating lace on the bag, a feature not shown by some contemporary artists; Morier, for example, shows just a plain lace edging. (Print after R. von Ottenfeld)

Emperor Joseph II, Maria Theresa's son who became joint ruler after the death of his father. In this contemporary print he wears the green uniform with red facings of his Chevauxleger regiment (no. 1), a favourite costume in which he often appeared.

Formed 1758 as part of Regt. Löwenstein (no. 31), made into a separate regiment under Prince Löwenstein (or more correctly Löwenstein-Wertheim) 1759, when Graf Saint-Ignon became *Inhaber* of the original regiment. Recruited in Moravia.
Uniform: grass green coat, red facings, waistcoat and breeches, yellow buttons (double row on waistcoat).

Carabinier Regt. No. 5 (or 1st Carabiniers)
Title: 1768 Sachsen-Teschen; alternatively 'Prinz Albert', Albert of Saxe-Teschen being *Inhaber*. Formed 1768.
Uniform: cuirassier style, white coat with dark red facings and collar-patch, and red lace on the turned-back corners of the waistcoat; yellow buttons.

Carabinier Regt. No. 6 (or 2nd Carabiniers)
Titles: 1768 Althann, 1770 Erzherzog Franz. Formed 1768.
Uniform: as Carabinier Regt. No. 5, but white buttons.

Hussars

Note: uniform-details are generally restricted to those worn *c.* 1762 unless otherwise stated; braid-colour indicates that worn on dolman, pelisse, breeches, boots and cap-lines unless otherwise stated. Later uniforms are summarised in the foregoing section. All regiments were raised in Hungary unless otherwise stated.

Hussar Regt. No. 2
Title: Kaiser. Raised in Slovakia 1756 by the Emperor Francis Stephen.
Uniform: see Plate E3.

Hussar Regt. No. 11
Titles: 1740 Csaky, 1741 Nádasdy (or Nádasti). The oldest hussar regiment, formed 1688.
Uniform: this regiment exemplifies the change of uniform and the conflict of contemporary sources. The uniform was red in 1726; Morier (*c.* 1748) may show this regiment with green dolman and pelisse, red breeches and yellow braid. In 1757 it kept dark green though blue was ordered, and two versions are recorded in 1762. One has a dark green busby-bag, dolman and pelisse, yellow cuffs, braid and buttons (three rows), dark blue breeches, yellow sash with green barrels or red with yellow, green sabretache with yellow edge, bearing yellow crown over black double eagle; Ottenfeld shows red cuffs. Another version indicates red busby-bag and dolman, dark blue pelisse and breeches, yellow braid and buttons (five rows), red sabretache with yellow undulating edging, bearing yellow crown over a black double eagle. Other descriptions refer to the uniform-colour as light green, and a slightly later chart shows the green dolman and pelisse with red breeches.

Hussar Regt. No. 16
Titles: 1740 Károlyi (or Carolyi), 1759 Rudolph Pálffy, 1768 Hadik. Recruited in Slovakia and western Hungary.
Uniform: in 1734 the regiment is depicted wearing light blue with red stocking-cap, dolman-cuffs and *scharawaden*, with matching light blue shabraque with red braid, yet in 1741 a Prussian source describes the uniform as light green, and Morier also shows it as green (see Plate E1). By the Seven Years' War blue is again recorded: blue dolman, pelisse and breeches, light red busby-bag and cuffs, red braid, yellow buttons (five rows on dolman, three on pelisse), red sash with blue barrels, light red sabretache with blue undulating edging, crown and double eagle. Other sources indicate white buttons.

Hussar Regt. No. 17
Title: Kálnoky (or Kálnocky); also known as *Siebenbürgisches Huszaren* (Transylvanian Hussar Regt.). Raised in Transylvania 1742.
Uniform: Morier shows dark blue busby-bag, pelisse,

dolman and *scharawaden* (over tan leather breeches), yellow braid, red sash with light blue barrels and red boots; but by the Seven Years' War the uniform included red busby-bag, light blue dolman and pelisse, yellow braid and buttons (three rows on dolman, five on pelisse), yellow sash with light blue barrels, red breeches, red sabretache with yellow crown over 'K' in wreath. Alternatives include dark blue pelisse and cap-lines; Ottenfeld indicates a light blue ground to the sabretache.

Hussar Regt. No. 24
Title: 1742 Paul Esterházy, 1762 Lusinszky, 1773 Wurmser. Formed 1742 in western Hungary, disbanded 1775.
Uniform: see Plate E2.

Hussar Regt. No. 30
Titles: 1740 Baranyay (or Baranyai), 1766 Nauendorff, 1775 Wurmser.
Uniform: see Plate G3.

Hussar Regt. No. 32
Titles: 1740 Dessewffy (or Desöffy), 1742 Festetics, 1757 Széchényi (or Szecheny), 1767 Ujházy, 1768 Emerich Esterházy.
Uniform: dark blue busby-bag, dolman, pelisse, breeches, red cuffs and braid, yellow buttons (five rows on dolman, three on pelisse), red sash with dark blue barrels, red sabretache bearing yellow undulating edging and yellow 'S' within crowned wreath.

Hussar Regt. No. 34
Titles: 1740 Havór, 1744 Dessewffy (or Desöffy), 1768 Ujházy, 1773 Graeven.
Uniform: red busby-bag, cuffs, braid and breeches, light blue dolman and pelisse with five and three rows of white buttons respectively, light blue sash with red barrels, black boots with light blue braid, light blue sabretache bearing red undulating edging, double eagle and crown.

Hussar Regt. No. 35
Titles: 1741 Beleznay, 1754 Morocz, 1759 Bethlén, 1775 Barcó; raised 1741.
Uniform: light red busby-bag, dolman-cuffs and braid, light blue dolman, pelisse and breeches, yellow buttons

(three rows), light red sash with light blue barrels; Ottenfeld indicates light blue busby-bag and white buttons.

Hussar Regt. No. 36
Titles: 1756 Batthianyi (or Batthyány), 1765 Török; but often styled as the Palatinal Hussars or Jazygier & Kumanier Regt. (or Jazyger & Kumaner); raised 1756, disbanded 1775.
Uniform: see Plate G2.

Hussar Regt. No. 40
Title: Carlstadter-Grenz-Huszaren (or 'Karlstädter'); a *Grenz* (border) corps formed in Croatia 1746, disbanded 1780.
Uniform: red busby-bag and dolman cuffs, dark blue dolman, pelisse, breeches, yellow braid and buttons (three rows on dolman, five on pelisse), yellow sash with white barrels, dark blue sabretache with yellow undulating edging, yellow crown over double eagle. An alternative indicates yellow cuffs.

Hussar trooper, c. 1748, attributed to either Regt. Beleznay (no. 35) or Ghilányi; a painting by David Morier, c. 1748. This includes an early depiction of the felt cap which could be worn as an alternative to the busby, here black with an unfolded 'wing' like a mirliton; green dolman and pelisse, red breeches and cloak, yellow braid and boots; red shabraque with yellow decoration. (The Royal Collection © 1993 Her Majesty the Queen)

Hussar Regt. No. 41

Title: Warasdiner-Grenz-Huszaren; a *Grenz* (border) corps, formed Croatia 1746, disbanded 1780.

Uniform: red busby-bag, dolman, pelisse, breeches, white braid and buttons, red sash with white barrels.

Hussar Regt. No. 42

Title: Banalisten-Grenz-Huszaren; a *Grenz* (border) corps, formed in Croatia 1750 by Count Carl Batthianyi; disbanded 1780.

Uniform: red busby-bag and dolman, dark blue pelisse and breeches, yellow braid and buttons, red sash with yellow barrels, red sabretache with yellow border, bearing yellow crown over black double eagle.

Hussar Regt. No. 43

Title: Slavonisches (or 'Slavonier' or 'Esclavonier') – Grenz-Huszaren; a *Grenz* (border) corps raised in Slavonia 1747.

Uniform: red busby-bag, dolman cuffs, breeches, green dolman and pelisse, yellow or mixed yellow and white braid, yellow buttons (five rows on dolman, three on pelisse), red sash with yellow barrels, red sabretache with yellow undulating edging, bearing yellow crown over black double eagle (Ottenfeld indicates green sabretache; the green of the dolman and pelisse is recorded as either dark or light).

Hussar Regt. No. 44

Title: Siebenbürgisches Székler; raised in Transylvania 1742.

Uniform: dark blue dolman and pelisse, red breeches; a later chart shows also yellow cuffs and sash, white pelisse-fur, and dark blue breeches.

Hussar Regt. Pestvármegyey

Titles: 1740 Pestvarmegyey, 1743 Trips; disbanded 1748.
Uniform: not known.

Hussar Regt. Splenyi

Titles: 1740 Splenyi (or Spleny), 1762 Emerich Esterházy; disbanded 1768.

Uniform: green busby-bag, dolman and pelisse, red dolman cuffs and breeches, mixed red and white braid, white cap-lines, white buttons (five rows on dolman, three on pelisse), red sash with green barrels, green sabretache with white edging piped red, bearing a heraldic beast upon a blue shield. Alternatives recorded include red busby-bag and light blue breeches, and the shade of green is recorded as either light or dark.

Hussar Regt. Ghilányi

Titles: 1740 Ghilányi (or Ghylany), 1753 Hadik. Recruited in Transylvania; disbanded 1768.

Uniform: see Plate F2.

Bibliography

Dr. H. Bleckwenn, *Reiter, Husaren und Grenadiere: Die Uniformen der Kaiserlichen Armee am Rhein 1734: Zeichnungen des Philipp Franz, Freiherrn von Gudenus* (Dortmund, 1979). Contains useful early illustrations.

C. Duffy, *The Army of Maria Theresa: The Armed Forces of Imperial Austria 1740–1780* Newton Abbot 1977 (latest ed. Doncaster, 1990). The most important work in English on the Austrian army of the mid 18th century, essential reading, with a comprehensive bibliography.

C. Duffy, *The Military Experience in the Age of Reason* (London, 1987). Provides an insight into the general conditions of warfare in this period.

A. E. Haswell Miller & N. P. Dawnay, *Military Drawings & Paintings in the Royal Collection* (London, 1966–70). Contains illustrations of David Morier's paintings, which are examined by Dr. H. Bleckwenn in the periodical *Zeitschrift für Heereskunde* (various articles, 1965–66).

F. Kornauth, *Das Heer Maria Theresias: Faksimile-Ausgabe der Albertina-Handschrift 'Dessins des Uniformes des Troupes, I.I. et R.R. de l'année 1762'* (Vienna, 1973). Provides important reproductions of 1762 uniform-illustrations, the 'Albertina MS'.

Richard Knötel, *Uniformenkunde* series of plates. Contains important reference to uniforms and equipment.

J. Mollo, *Uniforms of the Seven Years War* (Poole, 1977). Provides excellent coverage of the military costume of the period.

R. von Ottenfeld & O. Teuber, *Die Österreichische Armee von 1700 bis 1867* (Vienna, 1895). Remains an important reference on uniforms and equipment.

Hussar officer (left) and trumpeter, c. 1760; whereas the officer wears a more decorated version of ordinary regimental uniform, the trumpeter has a mixture of styles, including a 'German'-style coat and tricorn worn with Hungarian legwear and a braided waistcoat. (Print after R. von Ottenfeld)

R. D. Pengel & G. R. Hurt, *Austrian Dragoons, Cuirassiers 1740–1762* (Birmingham, 1982).

R. D. Pengel & G. R. Hurt, *Austro-Hungarian Hussars, Artillery & Support Troops 1740–1762* (Birmingham, 1983).

THE PLATES

A1: Trooper, Cuirassier Regt. Diemar (no. 33), 1748

This uniform, after David Morier, includes the singular cuff-flap, an item of costume which appears only rarely in Austrian uniforms. Although they were normally reserved for campaigns against the Turks, Morier shows the back-plate of the cuirass worn in western Europe; and his paintings show the cartridge-box with a belt so long that the box rests at

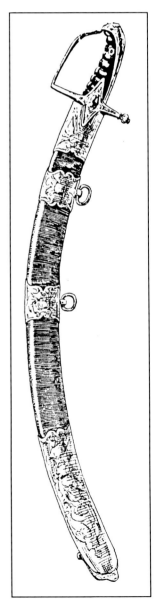

Hussar officer in undress uniform, illustrating the practice of wearing a braided coat and tricorn with more conventional items of hussar uniform. (Print after R. von Ottenfeld)

Hussar officer's sabre with decorated mounts. (Print after R. von Ottenfeld)

the rear of the rolled cloak. The regimental pattern of horse-furniture is typical, with the cross of the Teutonic Order on the shabraque.

A2: Trooper, Cuirassier Regt. De Ville

Regt. De Ville had red facings and breeches, white waistcoat, yellow buttons (two rows on waistcoat) and a red 'collar' patch across the top of the breast (there being no collar), a feature sometimes shown as a strip of facing-coloured cloth fastening together the upper breast of the coat.

A3: Cuirassier officer

Apart from the colour of waistcoat and breeches, regimental distinctions are concealed by the cuirass. This subaltern displays officers' marks of rank in the metallic lace on hat and waistcoat, the *Feldbinde* (waist-sash), and the gilt-ornamented cuirass. The cuirass has the minimum of gilding as appropriate for the lower commissioned ranks.

B1: Trooper, Cuirassier Regt. Alt-Modena

Regt. Alt-Modena was the only cuirassier corps to wear dark blue facings and breeches; white waistcoat, shoulder-strap and buttons (Ottenfeld indicates yellow buttons with two rows on the waistcoat). The man illustrated wears the carbine- and shoulder-belt, and is armed with a 1759 *Trombon* with the blunderbuss style bell-mouth.

B2: NCO, Cuirassier Regt. Bretlach (no. 29)

Regt. Bretlach had red facings, straw-yellow waistcoat and breeches, white shoulder-strap and buttons, and the unusual distinction of wearing a folding collar on the coat. NCO distinctions were generally limited to hat-lace and the cane, which was usually suspended from a coat-button when not carried; in addition, their weapons were often of finer workmanship than those carried by the other ranks.

B3: Trooper, Cuirassier Regt. Anhalt-Zerbst (no. 25)

This regiment wore red facings, straw-yellow breeches and waistcoat and yellow buttons (Knötel shows white breeches); the pattern of waistcoat was a singular distinction, with concealed fastening and red lace edging to the bottom and turned-back front corners.

Dragoons, c. 1760; the man holding the saddle wears the sleeved waistcoat and a cloth forage-cap. (Print after R. von Ottenfeld)

C1: Grenadier, Dragoon Regt. Liechtenstein (no. 6), 1748

Based on a Morier painting, this depicts typical élite company distinctions. The regiment wore a dark blue or violet coat and shoulder-strap, red facings and breeches and yellow buttons (double row on waistcoat, although Morier shows a single row, as does Ottenfeld, in white); light straw-coloured breeches are also recorded. The regimental grenadier cap is shown without a plate. It has been stated that the rear bags of grenadier caps were in the facing-colour, with button-coloured lace, but this rule was not universal according to some contemporary pictures. The horse-furniture is typical of the regimentally laced type used before the introduction of a universal pattern.

C2: Grenadier, Dragoon Regt. Batthianyi (no. 7)

Regt. Batthianyi is shown with a dark blue or blue-violet coat by the 1760s, but earlier it had a distinctly purple shade, with shoulder-strap, waistcoat and breeches the same colour, red facings and yellow buttons (double row on waistcoat). Morier shows a red waistcoat and breeches and, unusually, a curved sabre.

C3: Trooper, Dragoon Regt. Sachsen-Gotha (no. 28)

This regiment wore a red coat with light blue facings and waistcoat, straw-yellow breeches, and yellow aiguillette and buttons. The uniform exemplifies the many small variations which are encountered in various sources: for example, the 1762 Albertini MS shows a double row of buttons on the waistcoat, whereas the later reconstructions by Ottenfeld and Knötel show only a single row.

D1: Officer, Dragoon Regt. 'Savoyen' (Aspremont-Linden) (no. 9)

This famous regiment, associated with Eugene of Savoy, wore a red coat, shoulder-strap, waistcoat and breeches, black facings and yellow buttons (two rows on waistcoat). This shows a typical officer's uniform, the coat worn with skirts unfastened (thus without turnbacks), and an unlaced waistcoat; a contemporary portrait shows more or less this uniform, but with more buttons on the upper edge of the cuff (perhaps two groups of three), and a buff-coloured waistcoat with gold edging.

D2: Drummer, Dragoon Regt. Löwenstein (no. 31), c. 1758

This regiment wore a green coat with red facings and waistcoat, straw-yellow breeches and yellow buttons (two rows on the waistcoat); some sources indicate white buttons. Trumpeters and drummers (cuirassiers had kettle-drummers) were distinguished by 'swallows'-nest'-style wings, for which various designs of lace decoration are recorded; a plain example is shown here. Hat-lace is also often indicated. Drums are recorded as shown, with black 'flames' extending up the body; others are recorded with plain wooden shells bearing the Imperial arms.

D3: Trooper, Dragoon Regt. Hessen-Darmstadt (no. 19)

Apart from the Staff Dragoons, this was the only dragoon regiment to wear a coat without lapels; the

uniform included a poppy-red coat with green facings, yellow aiguillette and buttons, and straw-yellow breeches and waistcoat, the latter with turned-back corners and green edging. The waistcoat is recorded with a single row of buttons, but otherwise is shown to have concealed fastening, for example by Knötel and Ottenfeld.

D4: Trooper, Dragoon Regt. Althann

This was the only dragoon regiment to wear white prior to the general introduction of that colour for dragoons in 1767. The uniform included a white coat, waistcoat and breeches, red facings and aiguillette (some sources, including Knötel, indicate yellow aiguillettes), and yellow buttons; Ottenfeld indicates two rows on the waistcoat.

E1: Trooper, Hussar Regt. Károlyi (no. 16), c. 1748

Regt. Károlyi is usually recorded as having a light or dark blue uniform, but this figure is taken from a painting by David Morier, exemplifying the conflicting information that appears in contemporary and later sources. This is typical of the earlier hussar uniform, though without the scharawaden worn over leather breeches which appear in other Morier paintings, instead showing cloth breeches with elaborate braid decoration. Light coloured leather reinforcing appears not only on the elbows but on the side seams of the dolman. The shabraque is in a matching colour scheme, bearing the arms of Hungary at the front and those of the Inhaber at the rear; with the light blue uniform shown in the Gudenus drawing of 1734 the shabraque is also of a matching colour, light blue with red braid. Morier shows carbines carried with the butt in a boot at the right front of the saddle, but more commonly suspended from the carbine-belt. Large pipes also feature in some of Morier's pictures; the practice of carrying them stuck down the side of a boot is also illustrated.

E2: Trooper, Hussar Regt. P. A. Esterházy (no. 24)

The uniform of this regiment included red busby-bag and breeches, light blue dolman and pelisse, yellow cuffs, braid and boots, yellow buttons (three rows on pelisse, five on dolman), yellow sash with light blue barrels, and red sabretache with yellow undulating edging bearing a coronet over 'E' within a wreath, in yellow. Recorded variations include mixed red and white cap-lines and light blue busby-bag.

E3: Trooper, Hussar Regt. Kaiser (no. 2)

This regiment wore a dark blue busby-bag, dolman, pelisse and breeches, yellow cuffs and braid (five rows on dolman, three on pelisse), dark blue sash with yellow barrels or vice versa, and a dark blue sabretache with yellow edging (sometimes recorded as undulating) bearing a crown over cypher 'MT' in yellow. Some sources indicate the use of a very pale-coloured fur for the busby, even yellowish, and a buff-coloured *Czakelhaube* is shown in one chart, with white pelisse-fur instead of the usual black or brown.

F1: Trooper, Wallachian Grenz-Dragoons (no. 45), c. 1770

This was the only regiment of *Grenz* dragoons, and the only *Grenz* corps dressed in 'German' style, albeit equipped with small Wallachian horses and wearing hussar-style hair dressing, with plaits. The unit originally wore dark blue coats with crimson facings, white breeches, yellow buttons and Chevauxleger *Casquet*, but from 1767 they adopted the white dragoon uniform. Knötel shows red facings, although a later chart shows dark blue. The horse-furniture illustrated is basically that which came into use for heavy cavalry from the mid-1750s, with a universal design of shabraque and holster caps in place of the previous regimental lace and decorations; the holster-caps had a leather upper cover. Also shown is the 1769 disc-hilted sabre. Trumpeters of this regiment provide an example of the continuing use of contrastingly coloured coats; Knötel shows a blue coat with white facings and yellow lace, and a red-plumed, yellow-laced hat.

F2: Trooper, Hussar Regt. Hadik

Regt. Hadik (1740 title Ghilányi) wore a red busby-bag, dolman-cuffs and breeches, dark blue dolman and pelisse, yellow braid and buttons (three rows), red sash with yellow barrels, and a red sabretache with yellow edge, bearing a crown over a black heraldic beast upon a red shield with irregular yellow edge. White buttons are also recorded.

F3: Trooper, Dragoon Regt. Kolowrat (no. 37)

This regiment wore a dark blue coat with red facings, waistcoat and breeches, and white buttons (double row on waistcoat, although Ottenfeld indicates yellow buttons and a single row); this illustration depicts the rear of the dragoon uniform and the suspension of the carbine on the belt-clip, with a leather strap for additional security.

G1: Trooper, Hussar Regt. Kálnoky (no. 17), 1772

This illustration shows the hussar uniform intro-

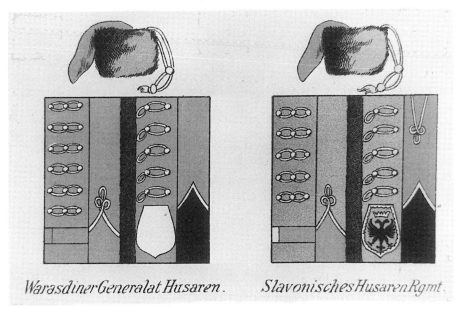

Hussar uniform, 1762; all red with white braid for Warasdiner Regt., green with red cuffs and breeches, red busby-bag, red and yellow sash, yellow braid for Slavonisches Regiment.

Warasdiner Generalat Husaren.   Slavonisches Husaren Rgmt.

duced from 1767, which specified a universal colour for dolman, pelisse and breeches. The universal yellow and black braid was worn on the uniform as well as upon the standard type of shabraque and sabretache. Shown here is the felt shako which replaced the busby for all except officers and *Wacht-meisters*, and the practice of wearing the pelisse as a jacket, a common fashion on service.

G2: Officer, Palatinal Hussars (no. 36)
The basic uniform of this regiment included a red or crimson busby-bag, dolman-cuffs and breeches, light blue dolman and pelisse with white buttons in five and three rows respectively, white braid, crimson or red sash with white barrels, and yellow boots. Officers' uniform generally included much finer materials; manufacture and metallic braid are often recorded as having a much more ornate application than for lower ranks. Similarly, officers' weapons were often finely decorated.

G3: Trooper, Hussar Regt. Baranyay (no. 30)
Regt. Baranyay wore a red busby-bag, green dolman

and pelisse, red braid, light blue breeches, yellow buttons (three rows on dolman, five on pelisse), red sash with yellow barrels and a green sabretache with yellow undulating edging, bearing a yellow crown over a black double eagle. A variation records yellow braid, but still red cap-lines.

H1: Trooper, Chevauxleger Regt. Löwenstein (no. 18), c. 1770
This shows the Chevauxleger version of the 1767 dragoon uniform, with a single-breasted coat in the distinctive colouring of green with red facings. Some illustrations show this pattern continuing to be worn unfastened, like the previous lapelled coat, revealing the waistcoat, latterly shown as green. The Chevauxleger *Casquet* was similar to that worn by the infantry, but taller. The horse-furniture is of the common pattern, and the sabre that of 1769.

H2: Trooper, Dragoon Regt. 'Savoyen' (Richecour) (no. 9), c. 1775
The 1767 dragoon uniform is depicted here, with the black facings of Regt. 'Savoyen', retained when both

the 1765 red uniform and the 1767 white were specified. Some sources do not indicate the retention of the aiguillette, but it is shown in some uniform-chart illustrations to the end of the period, in yellow (although not worn with the 1767-style uniform by the *Stabsdragoner* Regiment). The breech-loading Crespi carbine with its spear-headed rod-bayonet was issued throughout the dragoon and Chevaux-leger units. However, this weapon was withdrawn in 1779 after many men were burned during the War of the Bavarian Succession.

H3: NCO Trumpeter, Cuirassier Regt. Caramelli (no. 29), 1770

This illustrates the 1769 cuirassier uniform with single-breasted coat, musicians being distinguished by not wearing the cuirass, and often by a red plume. This illustration follows Ottenfeld in depicting the NCO sabre, a more ornate version of the 1769 pattern, with a gilded hilt and lion-head pommel, and a leather-covered scabbard suspended from a frog instead of slings. The NCO sword-knot is in yellow and black – probably universal by this date.

Hussar trooper, c. 1772, wearing the revised uniform, including a coloured felt cap and the universal design of shabraque and sabretache. (Print after R. von Ottenfeld)

Notes sur les planches en couleur

A1 L'uniforme est inspiré de David Morier et comporte le rare revers de manchette simple. Le harnais présente le motif régimental typique avec la croix de l'Ordre Tutonique sur le shabraque. A2 Reg. De Ville avait des parements et une culotte rouge, un gilet blanc, des boutons jaunes et un appliqué rouge en forme de col sur la poitrine (comme il n'y avait pas de vrai col). A3 Les marques du rang de cet officier sont la dentelle métallique sur le chapeau et le gilet, la cuirasse décorée de vermeil et le Feldbinde (ceinture de tissu).

B1 Reg. Alt-Modena était le seul corps de cuirassiers qui portait des parements et une culotte bleus, un gilet, une bandoulière et des boutons blancs. Notez le mousqueton et la bandoulière du soldat et le Trombon de 1759. B2 Regt. Bretlach avait des parements rouges, une culotte et un gilet jaune paille et des boutons jaunes. Notez les attaches cachées sur le gilet, la bordure en dentelle rouge en bas et les les coins retournés. B3 Regt. Anhalt Zerbst était le seul corps de cuirassiers.

C1 Le Regt. Leichenstein de Dragons portait un manteau et une bandoulière bleu foncé ou violets, un parement et un gilet rouges et des boutons jaunes. Le casque de grenadier est illustré ici sans plaque. Le harnais est de type régimental typique à lacets. C2 Regt. Batthianyi apparaît avec un manteau bleu foncé ou bleu-violacé à partir de 1760 mais avec un manteau, une bandoulière, un gilet et une culotte pourpre avant cette date. C3 Le Regt. Sachsen-Gotha de Dragons portait un manteau rouge avec des parements et un gilet bleu clair, une culotte jaune paille et une aiguillette et des boutons jaunes.

D1 Le Regt. 'Savoyen' de Dragons portait un manteau, une bandoulière, un gilet et une culotte rouges, des parements noirs et des boutons jaunes. Notez le manteau porté ouvert avec une jupe et le gilet non lacé. D2 Le Regt. LOwentein de Dragons portait un manteau vert avec des parements et un gilet rouges, une culotte jaune paille et des boutons jaunes. Notez les 'flammes' noires du tambour qui montent le long du corps. D3 Hessen-Darmstadt était le seul régiment de Dragons à part les dragons nationaux à porter un manteau sans revers. Le manteau était rouge conquelicot avec des parements verts, une aiguillette et des boutons jaunes et une culotte et un gilet jaune paille, ce dernier avec un passepoil vert. D4 Althann était le seul régiment de Dragons à porter du blanc avant l'introduction générale de cette couleur pour les dragons en 1767.

E1 Inspiré d'une figure de Morier. Ce soldat porte le premier uniforme hussard. Notez le shabraque assorti avec à l'avant les armes de Hongrie et à l'arrière l'Inhaber ainsi que les renforts en cuir auc coudes et sur les coutures latérales du dolman. E2 L'uniforme du régiment P.A. Esterhazy comprend un colback et une culotte rouges, un dolman et une pelisse bleu pâle, des poignets, du galon, des bottes et des boutons jaunes, une ceinture jaune et un sabretache rouge. E3 L'uniforme du régiment Kaiser comprend un colback, dolman, une pelisse et une culotte bleu foncé, des poignets et du galon jaunes, une ceinture et un sabretache bleu foncé.

F1 Le seul régiment de dragons Grenz, les Wallachiens étaient habillés en style allemand mais portaient leurs chevaux en style hussard avec des tresses. Le soldat porte l'uniforme blanc des dragons d'après 1767. Notez le sabre avec garde en disque de 1769. F2 Le régiment Hadik portait un dolback, des poignets à la fourragère et une culotte rouges, un dolman et une pelisse bleu foncé, des boutons et du galon jaunes, une ceinture et un sabretache rouges. F3 Le régiment Kolowrat portait un manteau bleu foncé avec parements, gilet et culotte rouge, des boutons blancs. Notez la manière dont le mousqueton se suspend à la boucle de ceinture.

G1 Cette illustration montre l'uniforme hussard de 1767 qui exigeait une couleur universelle pour dolman, pelisse et culotte. Le shako en feutre remplaçait le dolback pour tous sauf les officiers et les Wachmeisters. G2 L'uniforme de base des Hussards du Palatinat consistait en un dolback rouge ou cramoisi, des poignets à la fourragère et une culotte, un dolman et une pelisse bleu clair avec des boutons blancs, du galon blanc, une ceinture rouge et des bottes jaunes. G3 Le régiment de Hussards Baranyay portait un dolback rouge, une culotte bleu clair, un dolman et une pelisse verts, des boutons jaunes, du galon rouge, une ceinture rouge et un sabretache vert.

H1 Montre la version Chevauxleger de l'uniforme des dragons de 1767 avec un manteau à une rangée de boutons avec des parements rouges. Le harnais est de type courant et le sabre de 1769. H2 Simple soldat, régiment de dragons 'Savoyen' en uniforme de 1767 mais conservant des parements noirs. Notez le mousqueton Crespi à chargement par la culasse avec sa bayonnette à flèche. H3 Uniforme de 1769 avec manteau à une seule rangée de boutons. On reconnaît que cette figure est un musicien de par l'absence de cuirasse et de plumet rouge.

Farbtafeln

A1 Die Uniform ist David Morier nachempfunden und zeigt die seltene, einfache Manschettenpatte. Das Sattelzeug folgt dem typischen Regimentsmuster und hat das Kreuz des Deutschritterordens auf der Shabraque. A2 Das Regiment De Ville hatte rote Aufschläge und Reithosen, weiße Weste, gelbe Knöpfe und ein rotes 'Kragen'-Stück auf der Brust (die Uniform war kragenlos). A3 Die Rangabzeichen dieses Offiziers sind die metallisch glänzende Litze am Hut und an der Weste, der goldfarben verzierte Küraß und die Feldbinde.

B1 Das Regiment Alt-Modena war das einzige Kürassierkorps mit dunkelblauen Aufschlägen und Reithosen; weiße Weste, Achselklappe und Knöpfe. Man beachte den Karabiner und den Schulterriemen des Reiters und die 1759er Trombon. B2 Das Regiment Bretlach hatte rote Aufschläge, strohgelbe Westen und Reithosen, weiße Achselklappen und Knöpfe. Das Kennzeichen der Unteroffiziere waren der Hut und die Gerte, die an einem Jackenknopf hing, wenn sie nicht in der Hand getragen wurde. B3 Das Regiment Anhalt-Zerbst trug rote Aufschläge, strohgelbe Reithosen und Weste und gelbe Knöpfe. Man beachte die charakteristischen, verdeckten Haken an der Weste, die rote Litzeneinfassung am Rand und die zurückgeschlagenen Vorderecken.

C1 Das Dragoner-Regiment Liechtenstein trug eine dunkelblaue beziehungsweise violette Jacke und Achselklappe, rote Aufschläge und Reithosen und gelbe Knöpfe. Die Grenadiermütze ist hier ohne Schild abgebildet. Das Sattelzeug zeigt den typischen Litzentyp des Regiments. C2 Das Regiment Batthianyi wird Mitte der 60er Jahre des 18. Jahrhunderts in dunkelblauer beziehungsweise blau-violetter Jacke abgebildet, trug jedoch davor eine lila Jacke, Achselklappe, Weste und Reithosen. C3 Das Dragoner-Regiment Sachsen-Gotha trug eine rote Jacke mit hellblauen Aufschlägen und Weste, strohgelbe Reithosen und weiße Achselschnur und Knöpfe.

D1 Das Dragoner-Regiment 'Savoyen' trug eine rote Jacke, Achselklappe, Weste und Reithosen, schwarze Aufschläge und Knöpfe. Man beachte die Jacke, deren Schoß nicht zugeknöpft ist und die ungeschnürte Weste. D2 Das Dragoner-Regiment Löwenstein trug eine grüne Jacke mit roten Aufschlägen und Weste, strohgelbe Reithosen und gelbe Knöpfe. Man beachte die Trommel, die mit schwarzen 'Zungen' verziert ist. D3 Hessen-Darmstadt war außer den Stabsdragonern das einzige Dragoner-Regiment, das eine Jacke ohne Revers trug. Die Jacke war signalrot mit grünen Aufschlägen, gelber Achselschnur und Knöpfen und strohgelben Reithosen und Weste, letztere mit grüner Einfassung. D4 Althann war das einzige Dragoner-Regiment, das bereits weiß trug, bevor es 1767 als Farbe der Dragoner allgemein eingeführt wurde.

E1 Die Abbildung beruht auf einem Morier-Gemälde, und der Reiter trägt die frühe Husarenuniform. Man beachte die passende Shabraque mit dem ungarischen Wappen auf der Vorderseite und dem Wappen der Inhaber auf der Rückseite, sowie die Lederverstärkung an den Ellbogen und den Seitennähten des Dolman. E2 Zur Uniform des Regiments P.A. Esterhazy gehört die rote Husarentasche und Reithosen, ein hellblauer Dolman und der Mantel mit Pelzbesatz, gelbe Manschetten, Schnüre, Stiefel und Knöpfe, gelbe Schärpe und rote Sabretache. E3 Zur Uniform des Regiments Kaiser gehört die dunkelblaue Husarentasche, der Dolman, und der Mantel mit Pelzbesatz und Reithosen, gelbe Manschetten und Schnüre, eine dunkelblaue Schärpe und Sabretache.

F1 Das einzige Regiment der Grenz-Dragoner, die Walachen, waren im deutschen Stil gekleidet, hatten jedoch eine husarenartige Frisur mit Zöpfen. Der Reiter trägt die weiße Dragoner-Uniform, die nach 1767 üblich war. Man beachte den 1769er Säbel mit scheibenförmigem Heft. F2 Das Regiment Hadik trug eine rote Husarentasche, Dolmanmanschetten und Reithosen, einen dunkelblauen Dolman und Mantel mit Pelzbesatz, gelbe Knöpfe und Schnüre, eine rote Schärpe ind Sabretache. F3 Das Regiment Kolowrat trug eine dunkelblaue Jacke mit roten Aufschlägen, Weste und Reithosen und weiße Knöpfe. Man beachte die Aufhängung des Karabiners an der Gürtelschnalle.

G1 Diese Abbildung zeigt die 1767er Husarenuniform, die eine einheitliche Farbe dür den Dolman, den Mantel mit Pelzbesatz und die Reithosen vorschrieb. Der Filzschako ersetzte außer bei den Offizieren und den Wachtmeistern allgemein den Husarenkalpak. G2 Zur Grunduniform der pfälzischen Husaren gehörte eine rote oder karminrote Husarentasche, Dolmanmanschetten und Reithosen, ein hellblauer Dolman und Mantel mit Pelzbesatz mit weißen Knöpfen, weiße Schnüre, eine rote Schärpe und gelbe Stiefel. G3 Das Husarenregiment Baranyay trug eine rote Husarentasche, hellblaue Reithosen, einen grünen Dolman und Mantel mit Pelzbesatz, gelbe Knöpfe, rote Schnüre, eine rote Schärpe und eine grüne Sabretache.

H1 Hier ist die Chevauxleger-Version der 1767er Dragoneruniform abgebildet, mit einer einreihig geknöpften Jacke in rot mit grünen Aufschlägen. Das Sattelzeug entspricht dem allgemeinen Muster und der Säbel stammt aus dem Jahr 1769. H2 Reiter, Dragoner-Regiment 'Savoyen' in der 1767er Uniform, bei der jedoch die schwarzen Aufschläge beibehalten wurden. Man beachte den Crespi-Karabiner mit Hinterladung und dem Stangenbajonett mit Lanzenspitze. H3 Uniform aus dem Jahr 1769 mit einreihig geknöpfter Jacke. Die Figur ist durch den fehlenden Küraß und den roten Federbusch als Musiker zu erkennen.